What You Can Do About BREAST CANCER

What You Can Do About BREAST CANCER

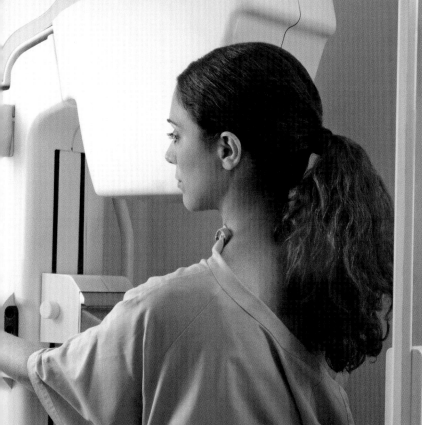

Don Rauf, Alvin and Virginia Silverstein, and Laura Silverstein Nunn

Enslow Publishing
101 W. 23rd Street
Suite 240
New York, NY 10011
USA

enslow.com

Published in 2016 by Enslow Publishing, LLC
101 W. 23rd Street, Suite 240, New York, NY 10011

Library of Congress Cataloging-in-Publication Data
Rauf, Don, author.
 What you can do about breast cancer / Don Rauf, Alvin and Virginia Silverstein, and Laura Silverstein Nunn.
   pages cm. — (Contemporary diseases and disorders)
 Summary: "Describes the conditions of breast cancer, the latest research, and treatment options"—Provided by publisher.
 Audience: 12-up.
 Audience: Grade 7 to 8.
 Includes bibliographical references and index.
 ISBN 978-0-7660-7032-5
 1. Breast—Cancer—-Juvenile literature. I. Silverstein, Alvin, author. II. Silverstein, Virginia B., author. III. Nunn, Laura Silverstein, author. IV. Title.
 RC280.B8R382 2016
 616.99'449—dc23
                          2015015539

Printed in the United States of America

To Our Readers: We have done our best to make sure all Web site addresses in this book were active and appropriate when we went to press. However, the author and the publisher have no control over and assume no liability for the material available on those Web sites or on any Web sites they may link to. Any comments or suggestions can be sent by e-mail to customerservice@enslow.com.

Portions of this book originally appeared in the book *The Breast Cancer Update*.

Disclaimer: For many of the images in this book, the people photographed are models. The depictions do not imply actual situations or events.

Photo Credits: Alila Medical Media/Shutterstock.com, pp. 37, 41, 44, 48; Alo Ceballos/GC Images/Getty Images, p. 88; Andrea Danti/Shutterstock.com, p 98; antoshkaforever/Shutterstock.com, p. 57; © AP Images, pp. 16, 18, 25, 27, 30, 54, 86, 100; Blend Images/Shutterstock.com, p 47; BlueRingMedia/Shutterstock.com, p. 39; Bork/Shutterstock.com, p. 63; Chicago Tribune/Tribune News Service/Getty Images p. 90; Classic Image/Alamy, p. 24; Dan Kitwood/Getty Images News/Getty Images, p. 96; David M. Benett/Getty Images Entertainment/Getty Images, p. 102; enterlinedesign/Shutterstock.com, p. 94; Glow Wellness/Getty Images, p. 1; GunitaR/Shutterstock.com, p. 43; © iStockphoto.com/fotostorm, p. 55; © iStockphoto.com/Mark Kostich, p. 70; Kevin Winter/Getty Images Entertainment/Getty Images, p. 33; © iStockphoto.com/powerofforever, p. 83; Mark David/Getty Images Entertainment/Getty Images, p. 9; Media for Medical/Universal Images Group/Getty Images, p. 50; Monkey Business Images/Shutterstock.com, pp. 59, 77; Orlando Sentinel/Tribune News Service/Getty Images, p. 53; Paul Morigi/WireImage/Getty Images, p. 35; Photographee.eu/Shutterstock.com, pp. 79, 81; polat/Shutterstock.com, p. 72; royaltystockphoto.com/Shutterstock.com, p. 21; science photo/Shutterstock.com, p. 65; Sebastian Kaulitzki/Shutterstock.com, p. 22; The Washington Post/Getty Images, p. 68; Tiffany Rose/WireImage/Getty Images, p. 13; vadim kozlovsky/Shutterstock.com, p. 60; WENN Ltd/Alamy, p. 104; William F. Campbell/The LIFE Images Collection/Getty Images, p. 73; ZUMA Press/Alamy, p. 93.

Cover Credit: Glow Wellness/Getty Images (mammogram).

CONTENTS

Breast Cancer at a Glance

WHAT IS IT?

Breast cancer is a disease in which breast tissue cells become abnormal and grow uncontrollably, possibly spreading to other parts of the body.

WHO GETS IT?

Both men and women can get breast cancer, but more than 99 percent of the cases occur in women. Breast cancer is more likely after age forty and most advanced cases are found in women over the age of fifty.

HOW DO YOU GET IT?

In most cases, the exact cause is unknown. In 5 to 10 percent of cases, it appears to run in the family. Other unchangeable factors may raise the risk of getting the disease, including age, race, and density of breast tissue. Some modifiable factors heighten the risk, including obesity, physical inactivity, eating an unhealthy diet, and alcohol consumption. Radiation therapy and hormone replacement therapy have also been linked to a higher risk of breast cancer.

WHAT ARE THE SYMPTOMS?

A lump in or near the breast or underarm may be a sign of breast cancer. At first it may be too tiny to see or feel, but a special X-ray called a mammogram may detect it. Any changes in the nipple (such as tenderness) or the breast (such as a change in skin texture) may be a warning sign. Sometimes there may also be a rash or a dimpling of the skin on the breast. Fluid may leak out of the breast.

HOW IS IT TREATED?

Often by surgery. The cancerous lump or the entire breast may be removed. Sometimes the underarm lymph nodes are also removed. Treatment with medications, radiation, or hormones may also be used. New targeted drugs can slow tumor growth.

HOW CAN IT BE PREVENTED?

A healthy lifestyle may help reduce the risk of developing breast cancer: Exercise regularly, eat a healthy diet and keep a normal weight, don't smoke, don't drink alcohol, and try to reduce stress. Limiting hormone therapy and exposure to radiation and environmental pollution may also lower the risk. Breastfeeding has also been shown to play a protective role. Drugs such as tamoxifen may be given to women at high risk to prevent breast cancer.

A Concern for All Women

In April 2014 Samantha Harris's career was going full speed ahead. The forty-year-old was living her dream. In college she had earned a degree at Northwestern University's Medill School of Journalism in Chicago, and now she was working as an entertainment journalist with the television show *Entertainment Tonight*. She had a string of successes. She had worked reporting entertainment news for *EXTRA, E! News,* and *The Insider.* For eight seasons, she cohosted the ABC hit *Dancing with the Stars.* She even fulfilled her dream of performing on Broadway by starring as Roxie Hart in the musical *Chicago.* On top of her busy work schedule, Harris was married and raising two young daughters.

She had always been passionate about fitness and maintaining a healthy body. While exercise had kept her fit throughout her life, she always had one nagging health concern. Her paternal grandmother had been diagnosed with breast cancer when she was sixty-three. (Fortunately, she had it treated and was still living into her nineties.) Her dad, however, was not so lucky. He was diagnosed with colon cancer at age forty-eight, and by

Samantha Harris has always made fitness and health a priority. This picture was taken in 2014, a few months before her breast cancer diagnosis.

age fifty he was dead. It was a devastating blow for Samantha, and she realized that her family history might put her at extra risk for getting cancer as well.

Samantha took extra care when it came to monitoring her colon health. In her mid-thirties, she started scheduling colonoscopies (a method for viewing inside the colon) every three years. Still, as she neared forty, she hadn't gotten an official breast exam. She felt healthy enough and was simply more concerned with colon cancer than breast cancer. Thinking about her grandmother, however, Samantha scheduled a physical and her first mammogram (an X-ray of her breasts) in April 2014. The doctors found her to be exceedingly healthy and her mammogram was clear.

Even with the clean bill of health, Samantha performed a breast self-exam eleven days after her checkup and found the unexpected: a lump.

She immediately scheduled visits with her ob-gyn (a physician focusing exclusively on obstetrics and gynecology) and her internist. They assured her that the lump was glandular. They told her she had nothing to worry about. But the lump did not go away. When the lump was still there four months later, she set up an appointment to see an oncologist (a cancer specialist).

The doctor performed an ultrasound and an MRI—both detailed types of screenings. Samantha also received a biopsy (taking of a tissue sample). All tests came back with good news—the lump was not cancer. The health experts, however, didn't know exactly what the lump was.

Then they removed the lump and performed further studies on it. She anticipated the same results. This time, however, the oncologist told her the shocking news—she had cancer. Samantha felt like she was hit with an anxiety attack. As with so many women who are told they have breast cancer, she felt her life changed in a second.

CELEBRITIES WHO HAVE HAD BREAST CANCER

Breast cancer affects people from all different backgrounds. Famous people are not immune. Here is a list of some people who have battled breast cancer, including one man. Although the disease is rare among men, they can get breast cancer as well.

ANASTACIA	SINGER
CHRISTINA APPLEGATE	ACTRESS
KATHY BATES	ACTRESS
PAT BATTLE	NEWS REPORTER FOR NBC
JUDY BLUME	AUTHOR
PETER CRISS	MUSICIAN (KISS)
SHERYL CROW	SINGER
MELISSA ETHERIDGE	SINGER
EDIE FALCO	ACTRESS
JANE FONDA	ACTRESS
PEGGY FLEMING	OLYMPIC CHAMPION FIGURE SKATER
KATE JACKSON	ACTRESS
PATTI LABELLE	SINGER
JOAN LUNDEN	TV HOST, *GOOD MORNING AMERICA*
KYLIE MINOGUE	SINGER
OLIVIA NEWTON-JOHN	SINGER AND ACTRESS
CYNTHIA NIXON	ACTRESS
SANDRA DAY O'CONNOR	FIRST FEMALE US SUPREME COURT JUSTICE
LYNN REDGRAVE	ACTRESS
ANN ROMNEY	WIFE OF POLITICIAN MITT ROMNEY
CARLY SIMON	SINGER
JACLYN SMITH	ACTRESS
WANDA SYKES	COMEDIAN

The next days, perhaps fueled by anxiety, her health changed. She felt restless and uncomfortable, and her stomach churned. The usually upbeat Samantha found it difficult to stay positive. She got several second opinions, but the diagnosis remained the same. The cancer was not going away unless she took steps to make it go away.

After visiting many specialists, Samantha narrowed down her choices to two to try and eliminate her cancer risk: She could either have a double mastectomy (removal of both breasts) or she could have another lumpectomy (removal of a lump) along with radiation. She decided on the double mastectomy. While in surgery, the doctors found that the cancer had spread to the lymph nodes and they removed them. Lymph nodes are masses of tissue containing white blood cells that help fight infections in the body.

In the summer of 2014, Samantha came out of surgery and began to regain her former energy level. She was declared cancer-free but she will have to keep up with checkups to make sure the cancer does not return. She will also take tamoxifen, which has been shown to block cancer-fueling estrogen, for possibly five to ten years. This drug has been show to have preventive effects when it comes to breast cancer and recurrence of cancer. After her surgery, Samantha returned to focusing on her exercise and healthy diet.

Realizing that support from others saw her through the ordeal, Samantha wanted to offer a way to support other women and men who might be facing adversity. She and her husband started a Web site called GottaMakeLemonade.com. On the site, people can share stories about how they "changed lemons into lemonade." The site encourages people to share their stories about obstacles they have faced and how they overcame them. Samantha hopes the site will inspire others to face challenges with a positive attitude and realize that there are ways to overcome these challenges.[1]

Samantha, seen here with her family, is now dedicated to supporting others facing breast cancer.

"You have breast cancer" is probably one of the scariest things a woman can hear. After hearing the diagnosis, many cancer patients start thinking about how much time they will have left to live. Cancer sounds really scary, but it doesn't have to be an automatic death sentence. Research has come a long way since the mid-1900s, when cancer was considered incurable in most cases. These days, the chances of surviving breast cancer are good, thanks to early detection methods and better treatments.

THE UNSPOKEN DISEASE GETS A VOICE

After heart disease, cancer is the second leading cause of death among women. Breast cancer is the second deadliest cancer among women worldwide—only surpassed by lung cancer. But even though breast cancer continues to be a serious health problem for women, the numbers are improving. Since 1990, the rate of deaths due to breast cancer has gone down by 34 percent[1] Early detection, improved cancer education, and advanced treatments have led to growing numbers of breast cancer survivors.

But for a long time, breast cancer was an unspoken affliction. In the early 1900s, cancer in general was viewed as incurable. People didn't talk about the deadly disease because it was thought that nothing could be done. The lack of education, awareness, and research about cancer in general were leading to increasing numbers of breast cancer deaths.

Attitudes began to change slowly, starting with the formation of the American Society for the Control of Cancer (ASCC) in 1913. The organization evolved into the American Cancer Society in 1945.

Mary Lasker was an early advocate for breast cancer research.

Still, cancer research was slow in coming. In 1943 Mary Lasker's housekeeper developed uterine cancer. When she checked with the ASCC to find our more about cancer research, she found that they did none.

"I became infuriated when I read that there was no single place which had as much as five hundred thousand dollars for cancer research," she said.[2]

As the wife of influential ad executive Albert Lasker, Mary began a ceaseless campaign to raise money for this much-needed research. But for many, cancer was still a word that people did not even want to utter. When she inquired about a fundraising campaign on the radio, Lasker was told that the word "cancer" could not be mentioned on the air. But she soon convinced the Radio Corporation of America that the time had come to mention cancer on the airwaves. She spread the word on the importance of early screening and detection. After her husband died of colon cancer in 1952, she lobbied the government to provide more funding for the National Cancer Institute. She felt her efforts reached a peak in 1971 when President Richard Nixon declared a "war on cancer" in his State of the Union address.

The 1970s were a time when women with breast cancer found a voice. Several prominent women of the decade publicly shared their stories, including Babette Rosmond, editor of *Seventeen* magazine; Shirley Temple Black, the child movie star and US ambassador; and First Lady Betty Ford.[3]

A NEW ERA OF SELF-EXAMINATION

When Gerald Ford took the oath of office as the president of the United States in August 1974, his wife, Betty, stood next to him. She supported him, as she had done through much of his political career. A month later, however, Betty Ford found out that she had breast cancer. Now she was the one who would need the support of her husband and family.

Betty Ford pictured outside Bethesda Naval Medical Center two weeks after having her right breast removed.

Betty Ford was fifty-six years old when she got her diagnosis. Her doctors had found a small lump in her right breast during a routine examination. (Around this same time, Happy Rockefeller, the vice president's wife, was also diagnosed with a cancerous breast tumor.)

On September 27, Betty went to the hospital for a biopsy. President Ford stayed by her bed, joking with her to keep her spirits up. The next day, they were told that the lump was malignant—that is, it was cancerous. Betty decided to have a radical mastectomy, in which the doctors would remove her right breast, some of the surrounding muscle, and the lymph nodes in her armpit. They found that two of the lymph nodes contained cancer cells, so she was treated with chemotherapy, powerful drugs used to kill any remaining cancer cells. The treatment turned out to be effective.

At the time, people were just beginning to talk openly about breast cancer, and Betty Ford was known for speaking her mind, especially on issues she cared about. She told the public that she had breast cancer and gave them details about her treatment.

Betty wanted women to know that breast cancer was an important health issue. It was not something they should be embarrassed about. She encouraged women to examine their own breasts regularly and get mammograms, which can detect the disease early.

Tons of mail poured into the First Lady's office, the American Cancer Society was flooded with donations, and thousands of women made appointments for breast exams. Betty Ford may have saved the lives of thousands of women, thanks to her openness and honesty about breast cancer.[4]

THE LONG HISTORY OF A DEADLY DISEASE

Breast cancer is actually an age-old disease that has been devastating women for thousands of years. In the past, treatments were often cruel and the effects were often deadly.

WHEN TO GET A MAMMOGRAM

The US Preventive Services Task Force recommends a mammography screening for women ages fifty to seventy-four every two years. The American Cancer Society, however, suggests that women start to have an annual mammography screening starting at age forty. Some women may decide to have a mammogram earlier based on possible symptoms of breast cancer or risk factors such as family history. The American Cancer Society recommends that women in their twenties and thirties have a clinical (doctor's) exam every three years. Ultimately, when a person chooses to have a mammogram is a personal decision and one to discuss with a primary care provider.

HOW CANCER GOT ITS NAME

Hippocrates, an ancient Greek physician, coined the name for cancer. He called the group of diseases involving tumors, lumps, and bumps karkinoma, *from* karkinos, *the Greek word for crab. Hippocrates thought the tumors looked somewhat like a crab, with their hard center and "legs" sticking out. (The "legs" are swollen blood vessels.) The Latin word for "crab" is* cancer.

The first descriptions of breast cancer were recorded as early as 1600 BC in ancient Egyptian writings. One author at the time wrote about "the cold bulging tumour of the breast." The only available treatments then were cutting out tumors with a knife (surgery) or burning them with red-hot irons (a technique called *cautery*).

Around 400 BC, Greek physician Hippocrates described cases of breast cancer. He wrote that tumors in the breast feel firm and continue to get harder. They do not contain pus, and they can spread to other parts of the body. These observations still hold true today. He also said that no treatment for hidden breast cancers existed, and that death was certain.

The first descriptions of breast cancer were recorded as early as 1600 BC in ancient Egyptian writings.

During the first century, Greek physician Leonides performed the first operation to remove the breast as a treatment for breast cancer. This operation is known as mastectomy. (*Mastos* is the Greek word for breast. The ending *-ectomy* means "cutting out.") Surgery was undoubtedly painful, since there were not yet any drugs to temporarily numb the body. In addition, doctors back then did not close up wounds by sewing stitches as they do now. Instead, they used cautery to stop the

The term *cancer*, which is Greek for "crab," comes from the appearance of the tumor. The Greek physician Hippocrates thought it resembled a crab. The breast cancer cell shown here also looks like a crab.

bleeding. They also did not have antiseptics, chemicals that kill disease-causing germs. As a result, the treatments often led to infection and death. Most surgeons at the time believed that it was better to leave the cancer alone.

SOLVING SOME OF CANCER'S MYSTERIES

During the early 1400s, scientists began to learn more about how the human body really works. Studies of animals and autopsies (surgeries performed after death) of humans provided a wealth of information. The invention of microscopes allowed scientists to discover cells, the basic building blocks of living things. Microscopes also allowed researchers to observe other body structures too small to see with the naked eye.

In the mid-1800s, German physician Johannes Müller reported that cancerous tumors were made up of living cells. These cells were abnormal, however, and looked different from normal cells. Müller also noticed that when cancer spread from the breast to other organs, the cells in the new tumors looked very much like those in the original breast tumor.

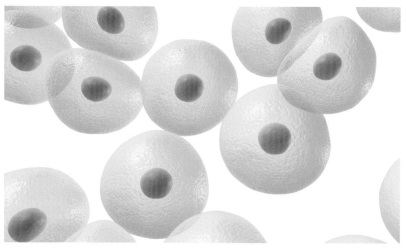

Healthy human cells, like the ones seen here, have many jobs throughout the body. Cancer cells develop from healthy cells.

CANCER WORKS ON A CELLULAR LEVEL

Your body is made up of trillions of tiny units called cells. Each one is too small to see without a microscope, yet a cell can do many things. It can take in food materials, produce energy, and send out waste products. Many cells are specialized to do certain jobs for the body. Nerve cells carry messages to and from your brain. Muscle cells are working each time you walk or run, throw a ball, or turn the pages of a book. Skin cells form a covering that protects your body's insides. The specialized cells of your body work together to keep you alive and healthy.

All cancers begin in cells. Cancers develop from normal cells, but the cells run amok and do not behave as they should. In cancer cells, messages telling the cells to multiply or to stop growing are altered so they may grow uncontrollably. As normal cells divide, it is a step toward cell death. But cancer cells in effect cheat death and have a way of rebuilding. In the right conditions, some cancer cells could live forever. Henrietta Lacks died of cervical cancer in 1951 at the age of thirty-one. Her cancer cells were preserved in a laboratory for cancer research, and they continue to grow today.

Joseph Lister was a British surgeon who promoted the use of sterilization in surgery.

A SURGICAL SOLUTION

In the mid-1700s, French surgeon Henri Le Dran suggested that surgery could actually cure breast cancer if it was performed early enough, before the cancer had a chance to spread. However, without anesthesia or antiseptics, surgery was not an appealing treatment. In fact, many women chose not to treat their cancer if it would involve surgery. The tools used for mastectomies were guillotine-like instruments designed to remove the diseased breast quickly, in as little as two to three seconds. The wounds were large and took a very long time to heal.

In 1846 Boston dentist William Thomas Morton was the first to use ether as an anesthetic during surgery. In 1865 British surgeon Joseph Lister discovered that carbolic acid was an effective antiseptic for killing germs. He started to clean wounds using a solution of carbolic acid. He eventually convinced other doctors to use the solution to wash their hands and to sterilize (make germ-free) surgical instruments and materials. With these discoveries, surgery started to become more popular. The procedure had become practically painless and relatively germ-free.

Even with the new techniques, however, the results of surgery were still not very good. Up to 20 percent of patients died as a result of infection. The rest of the patients generally did not live longer than two years after the surgery.[5] In 1867 British surgeon Charles Moore introduced the first "standard" mastectomy. He believed that methods of breast surgery that took out only part of the breast tissue might actually help to spread the cancer. Tumor cells that were left behind could travel to other parts of the body. Moore recommended removing the whole breast, as well as the lymph nodes in the nearby armpit and even chest muscles below the breast.

Surgeons in other countries soon agreed and began to use this method. One of them, William Halsted, was a well-known American surgeon at Johns Hopkins University in Baltimore. In 1894 he published a report that helped to make the "radical mastectomy" popular. In fact, it was so popular that doctors began to call this surgical procedure the "Halsted mastectomy."

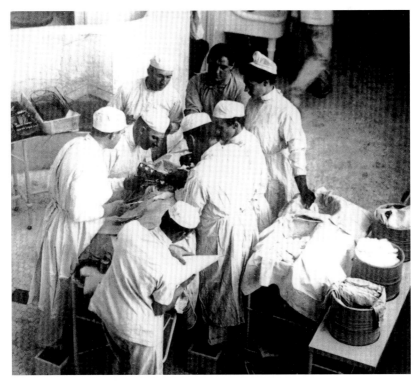

Dr. William Halsted (center left) operates on a patient at Johns Hopkins Hospital in Baltimore, Maryland. Dr. Halsted developed the first radical mastectomy in the late nineteenth century.

The radical mastectomy was criticized because removing the chest muscles not only left a huge scar but was often disabling. The procedure was so frightening that many patients would wait until the disease had become very serious to have it done. As a result, the Halsted operation did not really increase the survival rate—in many cases the cancer had already spread, and new tumors would soon appear. Nevertheless, radical mastectomy continued to be the "standard" treatment well into the second half of the twentieth century. (This is the operation Betty Ford chose to have in 1974.)

RADIATION AND OTHER THERAPIES

In the late 1890s new discoveries led to other treatment options for breast cancer. In 1895 German physicist Wilhelm Conrad Roentgen discovered a kind of radiation that he called X-rays. Using a special "X-ray machine," he was able to make a picture of the structures inside the body. He made his first photograph of the bones inside his wife's hand.

In January 1896 Emile Grubbe, a second-year medical student in Chicago, became the first person to use X-rays to treat a breast cancer patient. He got the idea after getting a radiation burn while experimenting with X-rays. The following year, Hermann Goeht treated two breast cancer patients with X-rays. All three patients had advanced cancer and died shortly after treatment. Researchers continued to study X-rays, trying to figure out safe doses of radiation.

In 1898 French chemists Marie Curie and her husband, Pierre, discovered radium. Radium is a radioactive element. Soon doctors started to use it to treat cancer. In 1906 British surgeon W. Sampson Handley suggested inserting a small tube filled with radon (a radioactive gas) inside the breast. The gas would destroy cancer cells that remained in the breast after a mastectomy. By the 1920s, radiation treatment had become widely accepted.

Marie and Pierre Curie discovered the chemical element radium in 1898. Radium began to be used in cancer treatment.

THE PROS AND CONS OF RADIATION

Radiation such as x-rays kills cells. In large enough doses, it can cause serious damage to the body. When radiation was first being studied, scientists did not realize this. Scientists Marie and Pierre Curie, for example, handled radioactive elements frequently, without wearing protective gloves or aprons. After years of doing this, they both became ill. Marie Curie eventually died of leukemia, a cancer of the blood. Pierre probably had leukemia, too, but he was killed in a traffic accident before the disease could be diagnosed. Their daughter and son-in-law, who continued their work, also died of leukemia.

In small amounts, however, radiation can be very useful in medicine. It is used in the treatment of cancer. In addition, x-rays can help to see inside the body and diagnose broken bones, tooth decay, and various diseases. (Marie Curie first suggested using x-rays for diagnoses during World War I, to locate bullets and shrapnel inside the bodies of wounded soldiers.) X-ray pictures of breast tissue, called mammograms, are used to detect tumors in the breast.

In 1922 English surgeon Geoffrey Keynes started to question Halsted's radical mastectomy. Keynes thought it was unnecessary and cruel. He suggested the removal of just the tumor along with a little bit of normal tissue around it. (This procedure was later called a lumpectomy.) He believed that this technique, combined with radiation therapy to kill any remaining cancer cells, would be enough. He treated many patients with early cancer, and found that over 70 percent of them survived at least five years.[6] Even though his results were encouraging, they were ignored by the medical community because the radical mastectomy was considered the "proper" treatment for breast cancer.

In the 1960s, long after Halsted's death, his theories and treatment were challenged once again. The radical mastectomy was based on the idea that a breast tumor gradually spreads into the surrounding tissues. A breast cancer specialist at the University of Pittsburgh, Bernard Fisher, had different ideas. In experiments on animals, Fisher found that cells from a breast tumor could spread through the nearby lymph nodes to other parts of the body, such as the brain or bones. The cancer cells settled in these other areas of the body and formed new tumors.

In 1971 a large-scale study began involving more than 1,600 women. Some breast cancer patients received radical mastectomies, while others had a "total mastectomy"—removal of the breast and some lymph nodes, without the surrounding muscle. Early results, published in 1975, showed that women who had only a mastectomy did just as well as those who had a radical mastectomy—and they had fewer bad side effects.[7] The medical community responded quickly. Soon the radical mastectomy was rarely used. The new standard was the "modified radical mastectomy"—removal of the breast and lymph nodes in the armpit.

After the early findings, the researchers based in Pittsburgh ran a study comparing the modified radical mastectomy with

Dr. Bernard Fisher testifies before the Senate Health Committee in 1976 at a hearing on breast cancer.

lumpectomy. Lumpectomy was sometimes combined with radiation treatments to kill any stray cancer cells. The new experiments showed that lumpectomy with radiation could be just as effective as the modified radical mastectomy in preventing the return of the cancer.[8]

DRUGS TO KILL CANCER CELLS

In World War II, a ship carrying a type of poison gas called nitrogen mustard blew up. Sailors were accidentally exposed to the poison. Doctors found afterward that these sailors had unusually low numbers of white blood cells, disease-fighting cells that are formed in the bone marrow and lymph nodes. Researchers thought that if nitrogen mustard damaged these organs and stopped white blood cells from multiplying, it might help in fighting leukemia, a type of cancer in which abnormal white blood cells multiply wildly. Later, poisonous chemicals were also used to treat other kinds of cancers, including breast cancer. This approach was called chemotherapy.

UNDERSTANDING BREAST CANCER

Rock-and-roll singer Melissa Etheridge amazed the audience as she sang a show-stopping version of Janis Joplin's "Piece of My Heart" on February 13, 2005. It wasn't the first time that Melissa had brought her fans to their feet, singing and clapping. But this was the first time she had sung in public since she'd announced that she had breast cancer.

At first, people were surprised to see Melissa walk onstage completely bald. Melissa didn't look sick, though—she was jumping around the stage, swinging her guitar and singing her heart out. This was not just an ordinary performance. This performance gave inspiration and hope to breast cancer survivors everywhere.

Just five months earlier, forty-three-year-old Melissa was shocked to find a lump in her left breast while she was taking a shower. It was a very large lump. She didn't know why she hadn't noticed it before. Not only could she feel it, but she could see it. It seemed weird how suddenly it had appeared. She had just had a physical that included a breast exam two

Melissa Etheridge performs in concert one year after her breast cancer diagnosis.

months earlier. She had been very good about checkups and self-exams because there was a history of cancer in her family. Her grandmother and aunt had both died of breast cancer, and her father had died of liver cancer.

Even though she was on tour, Melissa knew she had to get her lump checked out as soon as possible. She did one more performance in Ottawa and then flew back home to Los Angeles. When Melissa got home—just two days after her discovery—she noticed that the lump looked even bigger. She visited her doctor, who scheduled a biopsy right away. The day after her biopsy, Melissa was told that she had breast cancer.

Melissa canceled her tour and scheduled surgery so that the doctors could find out how serious the cancer was. During surgery they found a 1.6-inch (4-centimeter) tumor. They removed it. They also found that the cancer had spread to one of her lymph nodes. They took that one out and fourteen other lymph nodes, just to be safe: Breast cancer can spread into the lymph nodes and then through the bloodstream to other parts of the body. Later Melissa was told that she had Stage II breast cancer, which meant that it was in a fairly early stage. She was lucky.

Even though the doctors removed all of Melissa's cancer, the battle was far from over. She had to start chemotherapy ("chemo") and radiation therapy, typical treatments for cancer. She decided to shave her head even before she started chemo, since she knew the treatment would cause her hair to fall out anyway. Like other cancer patients who receive chemo and radiation, Melissa had a rough time dealing with the treatment. Some days it was a struggle just to get out of bed. Every part of her body ached. It hurt whenever she moved. She is very grateful to her family, who gave her the strength to get through it.

When Melissa was asked to sing at the Grammy Awards, she wasn't sure if she could do it. As soon as her chemotherapy treatments were over, however, she started to feel better. She

Melissa Etheridge attends a breast cancer awareness event. She has become a strong advocate for raising awareness of the disease.

was afraid that people might laugh at her bald appearance, but that didn't happen at all. In fact, it turned out to be an experience no one would soon forget.[1]

Now a breast cancer survivor, Melissa has changed her eating habits and lives a healthier lifestyle. Being on the road, she used to eat a lot of fast food. These days, she eats more salads and chicken. She also tries really hard to cut down on stress, which she admits has always been a big part of her life. Melissa now feels great and hopes to keep it that way. She is just as busy as ever. In addition to her career, she is involved in a number of efforts to raise breast cancer awareness.[2]

After skin cancer, breast cancer is the most common type of cancer that affects women. Although it usually occurs in women over the age of forty like Melissa, the disease can occur in younger women. The risk increases with age. A woman who lives for more than eighty years has a one in eight chance of developing breast cancer during her lifetime.[3] For men, the lifetime risk of getting breast cancer is one in a thousand.[4]

CANCER RISK RISES WITH AGE [5]

A woman's chance of getting breast cancer increases greatly as she ages.

Age 30	.44% (1 in 227 women)
Age 40	1.45% (1 in 68 women)
Age 50	2.29% (1 in 42 women)
Age 60	3.48% (1 in 28 women)
Age 70	3.88% (1 in 26 women)

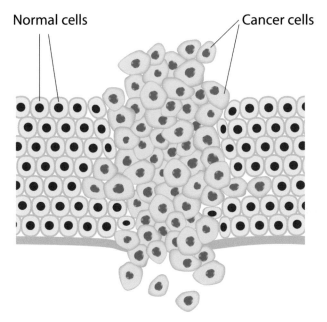

Normal cells   Cancer cells

Cancer (blue) cells in a growing tumor crowd out the healthy (red) cells.

HOW TUMORS DEVELOP

At some point, cancer cells keep dividing and can't stop. They creep over other cells and push their way into healthy tissues. They may pile up to form masses called tumors. Since the tumor cells do not obey the normal contact signals, they may invade other tissues, damaging normal cells and stealing the nutrients they need. Soon they start to choke out normal, healthy cells that have important jobs to do, such as making blood, digesting food, or controlling the movement of body parts.

Not all tumors are cancerous. Benign tumors are masses formed by cells that keep on dividing. They do not respond to the usual "stop" signals, but they do respond to contact with other cells. They may form huge tumor masses, but they do not invade other body tissues. If a benign tumor is removed, usually it will not form again. These tumors are generally not life-threatening.

> ***Not all tumors are cancerous. Benign tumors are masses formed by cells that keep on dividing. These tumors are generally not life-threatening.***

Cancerous tumors are often called malignant (harmful). Unlike benign tumors, these can damage the body. Cells from these tumors may invade nearby tissues. They may also break away from the main tumor mass and travel through the bloodstream or lymphatic system to other parts of the body where they may form new tumors. This spread of cancerous tumors from an original site to a new part of the body is called metastasis. If a malignant tumor is removed, some of the cancerous cells may be left behind. Even a single cancerous cell remaining in the body can begin to multiply uncontrollably, and the cancer comes back. The damage that cancerous tumors cause to various important organs in the body can lead to serious illness and death.

WHY THE BREAST IS SUSCEPTIBLE

Cancer is a group of more than a hundred diseases that have one basic thing in common: a change occurs in the body that causes cells to grow and multiply uncontrollably. The cancer cells choke out normal body cells and steal their food.

The type of cancer that develops is named after the part of the body where it starts. Breast cancer is a kind of cancer that starts in the breast. As the disease gets worse, cancer cells can spread to other parts of the body, most commonly to the bones, liver, lungs, and brain. Even if the cancer has spread to the bones, it is still called breast cancer, not bone cancer.

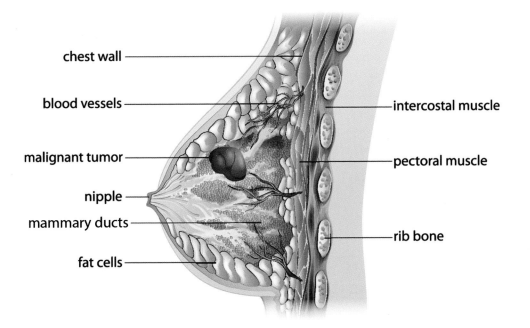

chest wall

blood vessels

malignant tumor

nipple

mammary ducts

fat cells

intercostal muscle

pectoral muscle

rib bone

This diagram shows the different parts of the breast and the formation of a tumor.

Cancer is a group of more than a hundred diseases that have one basic thing in common: A change occurs in the body that causes cells to grow and multiply uncontrollably. Breast cancer is a kind of cancer that starts in the breast.

Breasts are designed for one main purpose: to produce milk after a woman has a baby. Each breast contains lobules, tiny saclike glands that produce milk during breastfeeding. About a million lobules are in each breast. A collection of lobules form a lobe. There are fifteen to twenty lobes in each breast. When milk is produced, it is carried through hollow tubes called ducts from the lobules to the nipple. The lobules and ducts are surrounded by fatty tissue, which gives them support.

The breasts need a plentiful supply of blood to provide fluids and nutrients for milk production. The blood flows through a network of blood vessels. The smallest are capillaries,

CAN A HORMONE CAUSE CANCER?

Scientists have found that estrogen feeds breast cancer cells, helping them to grow and multiply. Therefore, they believe that the less exposure a woman has to estrogen during her lifetime, the lower her chances are of developing breast cancer. For example, the cancer risk is increased the earlier a female starts puberty and the later she starts menopause. (Menopause is the time during which a woman stops having her monthly period, and the ovaries no longer produce estrogen.) Earlier puberty and later menopause mean there are more menstrual cycles in a woman's lifetime. Thus, she has a longer exposure to estrogen. Hormone replacement therapy—taking sex hormones as medication after menopause—increases a woman's lifetime risk for breast cancer because of her longer exposure to estrogen.

The Lymphatic System

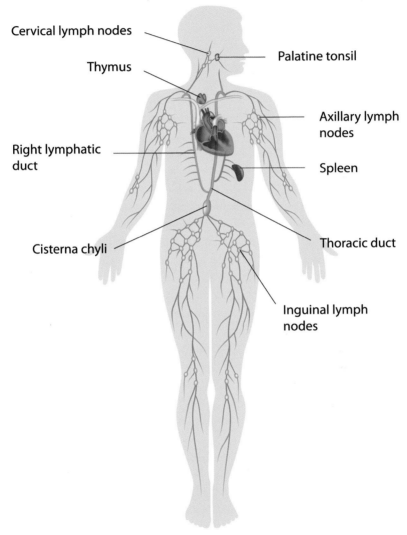

Cervical lymph nodes

Thymus

Palatine tonsil

Axillary lymph nodes

Right lymphatic duct

Spleen

Cisterna chyli

Thoracic duct

Inguinal lymph nodes

The lymphatic system is part of the circulatory system. One of its main functions is to protect against germs and cancer.

tiny blood vessels with very thin walls. The thin walls allow an exchange of water, nutrients, and waste between the blood-stream and the cells. They also allow fluid to leak out of the bloodstream into the surrounding tissues. This fluid, called lymph, includes not only water but also various blood proteins, salts, fats, and other materials.

Lymph fluid leaks out of the blood vessels all the time. Sometimes it builds up in the tissues and causes swelling. Most of the time, however, lymph is returned to the blood by another network of tiny tubes—the vessels of the lymphatic system. Lymph vessels drain fluid from tissues all through the body and empty it into large veins in the chest, near the neck. The main job of the lymphatic system is thus to manage the body fluids and help keep blood circulating.

The lymphatic system also has another important job: helping to defend the body against germs and cancer. In addition to the lymph vessels, it includes lymph nodes. The lymph nodes are small, bean-shaped structures where white blood cells gather. White blood cells are disease-fighting cells that help rid the body of infections. Lymph nodes are found in various parts of the body, including the armpits, neck, and groin. The lymph nodes in the armpits are called axillary nodes. The axillary nodes form a kind of chain from the underarm to the collarbone. Lymph from the breasts drains into the nodes in the armpits. When breast cancer is diagnosed, doctors usually biopsy these nodes to determine whether the cancer has spread to other parts of the body.

Chemicals called hormones affect the body in many important ways. They help to control chemical reactions in the cells. They also start and stop the growth and development of body parts and organs. The sex organs in both males and females produce sex hormones that act on other parts of the body. In a female, the ovaries produce sex hormones called estrogen and progesterone. In a male, the testicles make the sex hormone testosterone. It is estrogen that starts a girl's breasts growing during puberty. Estrogen and other sex hormones continue to act on the breasts for many years.

As a girl grows up, her breasts may go through changes in their shape, their size, and how they feel. Numerous milk-producing glands are formed during adolescence, so breasts often feel lumpy. (Normally, they will not produce milk until they are triggered by hormones released at the end of a pregnancy.) Adolescent girls have more dense (thick), glandular tissue than fatty tissue. Meanwhile, the body produces several kinds of sex hormones, including estrogen and progesterone. The amount of each kind rises and falls in a regular cycle, lasting about a month. This monthly cycle is called the menstrual cycle. The varying amounts of hormones (including estrogen) that are

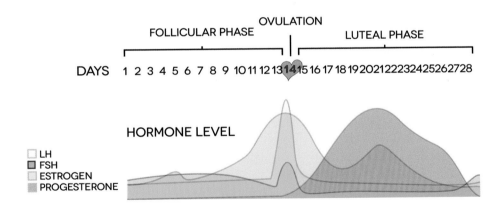

Levels of hormones fluctuate widely throughout the menstrual cycle, often causing changes in the breasts.

Mammary Ductal Carcinoma

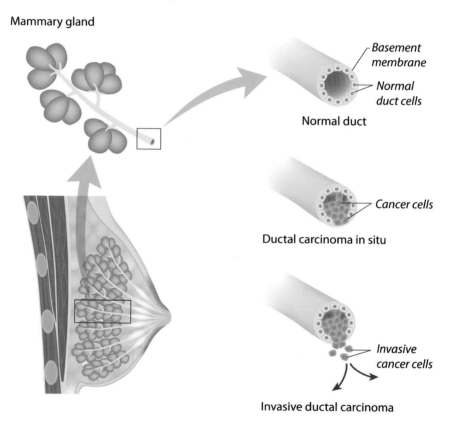

Mammary gland

Basement
membrane

Normal
duct cells

Normal duct

Cancer cells

Ductal carcinoma in situ

Invasive
cancer cells

Invasive ductal carcinoma

With invasive ductal carcinoma, the cancer cells have spread beyond their place of origin in the milk ducts and invaded surrounding breast tissue.

released during the cycle can make the breasts feel different at different times of the month. For example, breasts may feel lumpy and tender right before the monthly period.

Women may also feel lumps in their breasts during pregnancy and breastfeeding. These lumps are usually harmless—the glands get larger when they are actively producing milk. As a woman gets older, her breasts become fattier and lose some glandular tissue.

DIFFERENT FORMS OF BREAST CANCER

There are a number of different types of breast cancer. They can be put into two main categories: noninvasive and invasive.

Noninvasive cancer is also called carcinoma in situ. *In situ* means "in place"—the cancer has not spread beyond where it started. Noninvasive breast cancers are usually found in the ducts or lobules, and they have not spread to the surrounding tissues. Breast cancers in situ (especially those in the ducts) may later become invasive and spread to other parts of the body. But many women with noninvasive cancer in the lobules do not develop malignant tumors.

> *Breast cancer can be put into two main categories: noninvasive and invasive.*

Invasive breast cancers start in the ducts and lobules and then invade the surrounding normal, healthy tissues. They may also spread to other parts of the body, including the bones, liver, lungs, and brain. There are various kinds of invasive breast cancers, but invasive ductal carcinoma is most common. It accounts for about 70 to 80 percent of all breast cancer cases.[6] This type of cancer starts in the ducts of the breast. Cancer cells may then metastasize, or break away from the main tumor, and travel to the surrounding fatty tissue of the breast. The blood

THE RISK FACTORS

Even though the exact cause of breast cancer is not known, scientists have found that certain risk factors make it more likely that a person will develop the disease. Risk factors do not guarantee that a person will develop breast cancer—they just increase his or her chances. Here are some known risk factors for breast cancer:

• *Being a woman: Breast cancer strikes mostly women.*

• *Getting older: Breast cancer is most common in women over forty.*

• *Having a close relative, such as a mother or sister, who has had breast cancer*

• *Starting puberty before age twelve*

• *Starting menopause after age fifty-five*

• *Inheriting abnormal BRCA1 or BRCA2 genes*

• *Having two or more drinks of alcohol a day*

• *Being exposed to large amounts of radiation (such as X-rays or UV rays)*

• *Never being pregnant*

• *Having your first child after age thirty*

• *Smoking cigarettes or being exposed to secondhand smoke*

• *Becoming overweight as an adult (especially after menopause)*

• *Taking hormone replacement medication*

• *Poor diet that is low in fruits and vegetables*

and lymph can carry these cancer cells to other parts of the body, where they may cause serious damage.

HOW GENES PLAY A ROLE

How does breast cancer develop in the first place? Ultimately, it can be traced back to a person's genes. That doesn't necessarily mean that the disease is inherited. It just means that something has caused a change or mutation in the genes that control cell growth and division. The mutation is passed from one cell to another through cell division.

Every cell contains genetic material, called DNA (deoxyribonucleic acid). This substance is a complex chemical made up of smaller units joined together in various combinations. Parts of the DNA form genes, which carry the instructions that determine the characteristics of a cell and blueprints for making

Sometimes breast cancer is passed down through generations. Often this is due to the BRCA gene mutation.

new cells. The instructions are spelled out in DNA's chemical code.

To create new cells, body cells are dividing every day, every hour, every second of a person's life. When a cell divides, it splits into two "daughter" cells. These new cells are smaller versions of the original cell (the "mother" cell). The DNA replicates as well, so each daughter cell gets a complete copy of the DNA instructions its parent had. The daughter cells can then become mother cells to their own daughter cells, passing along the same genes they inherited from their mother, and the process continues.

When the genes in a cell are damaged, the defective genes are then passed on to future generations of cells. Some damages to genes can change a normal cell into a cancer cell. Usually these changes affect genes that control growth and cell division. Researchers believe that it takes a number of damaged genes to turn a cell cancerous. Generally it takes years before enough damage builds up to cause cancer.

WHAT LEADS TO DEFECTIVE GENES?

Scientists are not sure exactly what causes breast cancer. Many people think that it is inherited. This means the abnormal genes that may cause cancer have been passed on from the parents. Indeed, researchers have identified a number of abnormal types of genes that are linked to breast cancer. These genes, however, are found in only 5 to 10 percent of all women with breast cancer.

Many inherited cases of breast cancer have been linked to two genes: BRCA1 and BRCA2 (BRCA stands for breast cancer). Everybody is born with these genes, which are designed to suppress tumors. Normally, these genes help breast cells grow and protect them from becoming cancerous. When they are working correctly, they are actually preventing cells from growing out of control. But people who inherit a mutated form of either BRCA1 or BRCA2 will have greatly increased chances for developing breast cancer or ovarian cancer because the gene may not be able to repair damaged DNA.

About 55 to 65 percent of women with the BRCA1 gene mutation will develop breast cancer by age seventy. About 45 percent of women with BRCA2 gene mutation will experience the same. On the other hand, about 12 percent of women in the general population (without these mutations) will develop breast cancer sometime during their lives.[7]

Other gene mutations have been linked to breast cancer but are not as common as BRCA1 and BRCA2 mutations. Some of these genes are ATM, p53, CHEK2, PTEN, CDH1, and PALB2, to name a few.

Cases of inherited breast cancer are more likely to develop in women who have close family relatives with the disease, such as a mother or sister. The risk is also increased if a grand-mother or aunt has had breast cancer. However, a family history of breast cancer does not guarantee that a person will develop the disease. Moreover, most women with breast cancer have had no family members with the disease. In the majority of cases, other influences are involved.

OTHER GENE-ALTERING CAUSES

Chemicals called carcinogens can cause changes in DNA that may lead to cancer. Studies have found that carcinogens in the environment—radiation and chemicals in things that people eat, drink, breathe, or come in contact with in their daily life—may play a large role. Radiation, such as that given off by radioactive minerals, X-rays, and even the ultraviolet rays in sunlight, may damage genes and lead to cancer. Cancer-causing chemicals can be found in cigarettes, certain foods, and build-ing materials.

A number of studies have shown that obesity (being extremely overweight) in adulthood, especially after menopause,

Smoking has been shown to increase a woman's risk of developing breast cancer.

may lead to cancer. Fat tissue produces estrogen. So even after the ovaries have stopped producing estrogen, obese women's bodies are still making the hormone. The continued exposure to the hormone increases their risk of developing breast cancer.

A diet that is low in fruits and vegetables could also lead to cancer. Many fruits and vegetables contain important chemicals that may have cancer-inhibiting properties.

The Mayo Clinic lists other risk factors, including starting menopause at an older age, having a first child after age thirty-five, having never been pregnant, and drinking alcohol.

It seems that there is no single cause for breast cancer. Usually a combination of factors is involved.

Chapter 4

DETECTING, THEN TREATING

At age thirteen, Dakoda Dowd was a golfing phenomenon. As a young child, she had watched her dad play golf. When she picked up a club and tried a golf swing at age four, her father was amazed. She drove a ball far across a field. Golf seemed to come naturally to Dakoda, and she loved the sport. With a professional golf coach advising her, Dakoda entered junior golf tournaments and showed her star quality. She won more than 185 trophies. But in 2002, Dakoda started to lose her focus on golf. She had a new focus in her life: Her mom was diagnosed with breast cancer. Suddenly, spending time with her mom seemed more important.

Dakoda's mom, Kelly Jo, was thirty-six years old when she got the diagnosis. She had first discovered a lump in her right breast in December 2001. Her doctor told her it was probably nothing to worry about, but that she should get a mammogram anyway. Kelly Jo was so busy that she put off getting the test for months. When she finally got around to it ten months later, her doctor diagnosed breast cancer. Kelly Jo decided to get a double

Dakoda Dowd makes a putt at a tournament in 2006. Dakoda's mother was diagnosed with breast cancer in 2002.

Dakoda inspired her mom, Kelly Jo, to keep fighting breast cancer.

mastectomy. Twenty lymph nodes were also removed; two of them were cancerous. Afterward, Kelly Jo had chemotherapy and radiation treatments, and dealt with the usual side effects: hair loss, weight loss, dry skin, and extreme tiredness and weakness. Dakoda, who shares a very close bond with her mom, was there for her every step of the way. Kelly Jo admitted that she really didn't think she could have fought the cancer, but her daughter gave her the strength to get through it.

Kelly Jo started to feel well again. She went back to work, and her hair grew back. Then in May 2005, she started to feel achy. She thought it was due to exercising. Near the end of the month, however, a bone scan revealed that her cancer had spread to her hip bone and her liver. She now had Stage IV cancer—the most advanced and least treatable kind. The doctors told her that she had six months to a year to live.

Kelly Jo did not think she had enough strength to go through more chemotherapy, but her daughter convinced her. She would do it for Dakoda. Meanwhile, even though spending time with her mom was her number one priority, Dakoda never stopped playing golf. Kelly Jo didn't want her to stop.

The first step a woman needs to take after finding a lump in her breast is to schedule a medical examination.

Dakoda's dream was to have her mom live to see her play against pro golfers at the LPGA (Ladies Professional Golf Association) tournament in the Ginn Clubs & Resorts near Orlando, Florida, scheduled in April 2006. That would be nearly a year after Kelly Jo had been told she had up to a year to live.

Kelly Jo went through more chemotherapy, this time using different drugs that had less severe side effects. She was well enough to see her daughter play in the LPGA tournament. Kelly Jo was so proud. The mother-daughter team decided to talk to reporters about Kelly Jo's illness. They wanted to let people know how important it is to detect breast cancer early, before it's too late. She told them how she wished she hadn't waited so long to be tested after she felt her lump. Their new focus was to raise breast cancer awareness among the public and to help raise money for research. Unfortunately, even though Kelly Jo put up such a fierce fight against the cancer, she died on May 24, 2007. The cancer had spread to her brain. She was just forty-two years old.[1, 2]

LEARNING TO SELF-EXAMINE

When you have a cold, you may cough and sneeze and have a stuffy nose. You know that you are sick. With breast cancer, usually no obvious symptoms present themselves in its early stages. Still, early detection may be key to stopping cancer before it becomes fatal. Medical experts say the best way to catch breast cancer early is to do regular breast self-exams, or BSEs. This is a breast exam that a woman gives herself at home.

Medical experts say the best way to catch breast cancer early is to do regular breast self-exams, or BSEs.

THE BREAST SELF-EXAM

The American Cancer Society recommends taking the following steps to conduct a breast self-exam. The organization advises conducting this exam when breasts are not tender or swollen. Also, it's advisable to review your self-exam technique with a healthcare professional to make sure you're doing it correctly.

1) LIE DOWN ON BACK
Undressed from the waist up, lie down and place your right arm behind your head. Lying down allows the breast tissue to spread evenly over the chest. This position makes it easier to feel all the breast tissue.

2) CAREFULLY FEEL BREAST
Using small circular motions, run the finger pads of your three middle fingers on your left hand over your right breast. Use three different type of pressure to get a full assessment. Light pressure gives a sense of tissue closest to the skin. Medium pressure lets one feel a little deeper into the breast. Very firm pressure gives a sense of the area closest to the chest and ribs. Take notice: Are there any unusual lumps that weren't there before? Is there something hard, like a marble, or a lump with a strange shape?

3) BE THOROUGH
Examine up to the collarbone, out to the armpit, in to the middle of the chest, and down to the bottom of the rib cage. Repeat the procedure for the left breast, using the right hand for the exam.

4) EVALUATE LOOK OF BREASTS IN MIRROR
Stand in front of a mirror. Press hands firmly down on hips—this contracts chest wall muscles and accentuates any changes. Look at breasts and take note of any changes in color, size, shape, and contour. Look for dimpling, redness, or scaliness around nipple or on breast skin.

5) CHECK UNDERARM
While standing or sitting upright, feel under arm with arm slightly raised. Then raise arm straight up and feel again under arm with skin stretched tight.

Women should start doing BSEs around twenty years old, according to the American Cancer Society. That way they can become familiar with their breasts—how they look and how they feel. Then as they grow older, they will know when something doesn't look or feel right. Young women who have never done a BSE before might be surprised to find that their breasts feel a little lumpy, rather than smooth. As mentioned earlier, this lumpiness is usually breast tissue—and it is perfectly normal. A BSE should be done at least once a month, around the same time. A good time to do it is about a week after the monthly period starts. This is when the breasts are the least likely to be lumpy. They are also less likely to be swollen or tender. The instructions on page 57 describe how to do a BSE.

What if you do find a strange lump? Fortunately, most lumps—about 80 percent of them—are benign (not cancerous).[3] Benign breast lumps usually have smooth edges and move a little if they are pushed. For some women, the hormonal ups and downs during their menstrual cycle can cause changes in their breast tissue. These changes are known as fibrocystic breast changes. At least half of all women have these changes. They develop lumps in both breasts, which become tender and swollen right before their period. The lumps are actually milk ducts and surrounding tissues that grow and expand to form fluid-filled sacs called cysts. Fibrocystic changes are actually the most common cause of benign breast lumps among women between ages thirty-five and fifty. Fibrosis is firmness in the connective tissues and cysts are fluid-filled sacs.

Fortunately, most lumps—about 80 percent of them—are not cancerous.

Finding a strange lump in the breast can be scary for any woman. But when it comes to breast cancer, what you don't

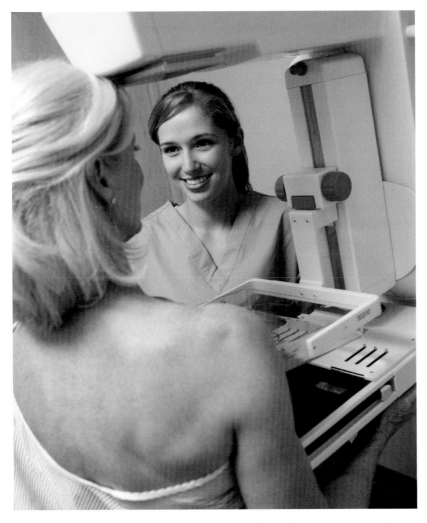

This woman is having a mammogram done. A mammogram is an x-ray of the breast.

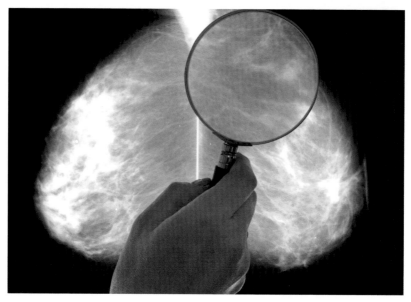

A doctor examines the results of a mammogram.

know can hurt you. It is important to get any unusual lump checked out by a doctor.

The doctor will first gather information about the patient's medical history, including any family history of breast cancer. Then the patient will be given a clinical exam, which is like a breast self-exam, but it is done by a doctor. The next step involves tests that can make an accurate diagnosis.

SCREENING AND TESTING

A mammogram is an effective tool for detecting breast cancer. This test is basically an X-ray of the breast. X-rays pass through soft tissue more easily than through dense (thick) tissue, such as bone. Typically tumors are rather dense and show up against the soft tissues around them. Like bones, these tumors will appear white on the X-ray film, and the neighboring tissues will appear darker. Some tumors, however, are not as dense as the surrounding tissue, or they may be very small, so they do

POSSIBLE WARNING SIGNS

In its early stages, breast cancer may not cause pain or any symptoms at all. As the disease develops, however, there may be noticeable changes in the breast or underarm. Possible signs and symptoms of breast cancer may include the following:

• Lumps in the breast. They may be hard or soft, and their edges may be rounded or uneven.
• A lump or enlarged lymph nodes in the underarm area.
• Swelling of part of the breast. Breast pain or tenderness.
• Dimpling of the breast.
• Nipple pain or nipple turning inward.
• Redness or scaling of the nipple or breast skin. Orange peel-like texture of skin.
• Fluid other than breast milk leaking out of the nipple.
• Unexplained weight loss of ten pounds or more.

Anyone who has some or all of these signs and symptoms should see a doctor.

not show up on the film. In addition, tumors may be missed in women with very dense breast tissue. So even though mammograms have been used to detect many cases of breast cancer, they are not foolproof.

The standard mammogram takes two X-ray pictures of the breast from different angles. A new type of technology is becoming more available called 3-D mammography (or breast tomosynthesis). This new technology takes many low-radiation images as the scanner moves over the breast. The computer translates the images into a 3-D image of the breast. It can provide a clearer view inside the body than the standard mammogram. In 2014 a study found that 3-D mammography can spot abnormalities that standard imaging may miss. This research showed a 29 percent increase in detection of all breast cancers.[4] The National Cancer Institute says, however, that it is not clear if 3-D mammography is better than standard mammography when it comes to false-positive results.[5] Some screenings will indicate that a person has a disease when he or she actually does not have the disease. This is called a false positive.

A mammogram is an effective tool for detecting breast cancer. This test is basically an X-ray of the breast.

Calcifications—small deposits of calcium—are mostly benign but sometimes they are an early warning sign of breast cancer. They look like grains of sand, and because they are so small, they are commonly seen in breast X-rays. There are two categories of calcifications—macrocalcifications and microcalcifications. Macrocalcifications show up on mammograms as large white dots or dashes. They are harmless and occur naturally as women age. Microcalcifications appear as fine white specks on a mammogram. Typically, these are not signs of cancer but sometimes a grouping of these in one area can be pre-cancerous. The radiologist (a doctor who analyzes X-ray images) will advise which calcifications may indicate a cancerous tumor and need to be studied further. (Note that these calcifications have nothing to do with how much calcium a person has in her diet.)

If the mammogram shows a suspicious lump or calcification, the doctor may order additional tests. One test may be an ultrasound. In an ultrasound, reflected sound waves are used to produce images of structures inside the human body. Sound waves are sent into the body via a small microphone-like device called a transducer, which is placed on the skin. The

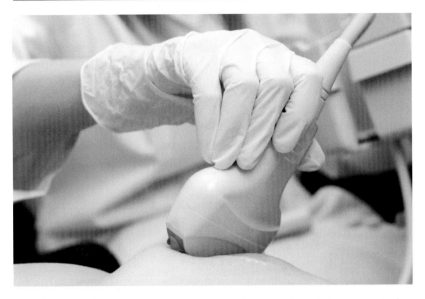

In a breast ultrasound, a transducer (shown here) is moved along the breast. It is able to turn sound waves into images on a computer screen.

high-frequency sound waves bounce off various structures inside, forming "echoes." The way the sound waves bounce gives information about the size, shape, and density of the internal structures. A computer turns this information into a detailed image, called a sonogram. An ultrasound can determine whether the mass is a fluid-filled cyst or a solid tumor. (In women who are under thirty years old and have breast cancer symptoms, both ultrasound and mammography may be used because they tend to have dense breast tissue.)

Another diagnostic test is the CT scan or CAT (computerized axial tomography) scan. This method uses tiny streams of X-rays sent through the body at various angles to produce pictures that are far clearer and more detailed than an ordinary X-ray image. The CT scan can detect tumors in such internal organs as the brain, lungs, and pancreas. It can provide valuable information about the tumor's exact location, size, and type. However, it cannot detect very small tumors, and it may not show where the cancer has spread.

An MRI (magnetic resonance imaging) scan uses a strong magnetic field and radio waves that pass through the body. It can produce clear images of almost any organ in the body. An MRI scan is more sophisticated than a CT scan. It provides better pictures and is better able to identify certain tumors. However, it doesn't show calcifications as well as an ordinary X-ray or CT scan. An MRI can be helpful in identifying breast cancers in dense breasts, but it is not a replacement for mammograms.

TESTING THE TISSUE ITSELF

If diagnostic testing shows a solid tumor, a biopsy is needed to determine whether the mass is benign or malignant. In a biopsy, a healthcare professional takes a tissue sample after numbing the area to be biopsied. In a needle biopsy, a long hollow needle is used to remove fluid and a small tissue sample from the tumor or mass. A technician then examines the sample under a microscope and checks for cancer cells. Usually this procedure will show whether or not the tumor is cancerous.

In some cases, however, the doctor may prefer to go beyond a needle biopsy and perform a surgical biopsy. This may be the best option if the tumor is harder to locate—for example, near the ribs or armpit. In a surgical biopsy, either the entire lump or part of it is removed, along with some surrounding tissues.

A nipple discharge exam is another possible testing route whereby the health professional collects the fluid and examines it for cancerous cells under a microscope. Women at high risk of cancer may also consider ductal lavage and nipple aspiration—procedures that draw out fluid for testing.

Based on the cells tested, a pathology report is created. The pathology report provides a diagnosis and information that

After a biopsy sample is taken, a scientist examines the cells under a microscope.

may include cell sample description and how it compares to normal cells, tumor type, stage of possible cancer, genetic information on the cells, and physical and chemical characteristics that may help with treatment.

After a diagnosis is made, some tests may help to show whether the cancer has metastasized (spread to other parts of the body), and if it has, where. Chest X-rays are used to see whether the cancer has spread to the lungs. A blood test may be taken to see whether the cancer has traveled to the liver. A bone scan may be used to see if the cancer has spread to the bones.

Certain tests may help the doctor understand more about the cancer, which can help in determining the treatment. A pathology report typically includes results from a hormone receptor assay (test). This hormone receptor test shows whether hormones (estrogen and progesterone) are helping the cancer to grow. If the test is positive, then hormone therapy may work to fight the cancer. (Hormone therapy involves drugs that will starve the cancer of the key hormones—slowing or stopping cancer growth.) If the test shows the patient to be hormone-receptor-negative, hormone therapy is very unlikely to help.

THE DIFFERENT STAGES OF CANCER

Diagnostic testing is used not just for detecting cancer, but also for "staging" the disease. Staging is a process that determines how serious the cancer is, where it is located, and how far it has spread. The cancer stage tells a patient and doctor about the extent and severity of the disease. The stage will determine the course of treatment. There are five stages, from 0 to IV. The higher the number, the more serious the condition. A Stage 0 cancer is a single tumor that is still small and has not spread to any lymph nodes or other organs. Stage IV cancer is the most advanced and most difficult to treat.

To stage solid tumors, the doctor examines the size of the tumor, the lymph nodes affected, and where the cancer has spread. A number of tests may be used for staging. These may include X-rays, MRIs, CT (or CAT) scans, and others mentioned earlier.

The TNM system is commonly used for staging cancers. It includes three important elements: *T* refers to the size of the tumor and whether it has invaded nearby tissues and organs. *N* describes whether the cancer has spread to nearby lymph nodes, and if so, how far it has spread along the lymphatic system. *M* indicates whether the cancer has spread to other organs in the body, forming new tumors (metastasis), and if so, how many organs are involved.

Once the TNM values have been determined, they are combined into a more general classification to indicate the stage of the cancer—whether it be 0, I, II, III, or IV.

DETERMINING THE MOST EFFECTIVE THERAPY

Surgery is one treatment option that works best when the cancer is discovered early. If a tumor is cut out before it has metastasized, the patient can be completely cured. The surgeon must try to get out all of the cancer cells. That means taking out some of the normal tissues that the cancer may have invaded, and possibly lymph nodes as well. If any cancer cells are left, they can begin to multiply again after the operation. Imagine this: A tumor the size of your thumb contains one billion malignant cells. If an operation removed 99.9 percent of the tumor, there would still be one million cancer cells left.

To make sure that all the cancer is removed, surgeons are concerned with tumor margins. They examine the tissue microscopically to make sure they're getting all cancer out of they body. The margin is the edge of the tissue that has been removed. A clear margin (also called clean or negative) means that no cancer cells have been detected at the outer edge of the removed tissue. A positive margin means that cancer cells are coming to the edge of the surgically extracted tissue, and more surgery will probably be needed. A close margin diagnosis means the cancerous cells are very close to the edge—doctors have to carefully evaluate this situation and determine if additional surgery is required.

There are basically two types of surgery for breast cancer: lumpectomy and mastectomy. In a lumpectomy, the surgeon cuts out the tumor and some normal breast tissue around it. Lymph nodes may also be removed from the armpit. In a mastectomy, the entire breast is removed. Rarely, some women need a double mastectomy—the removal of both breasts—to prevent cancer from developing in the other breast.

There are basically two types of surgery for breast cancer: lumpectomy and mastectomy.

This breast surgeon is explaining treatment options to a new patient.

In a lumpectomy, the surgeon cuts out the tumor.
In a mastectomy, the entire breast is removed.

Getting a mastectomy can greatly affect how a woman feels about herself. Losing one or both breasts can be shocking and upsetting. Many women choose to have breast reconstruction to restore the look and feel of their breasts. One popular option is to have implants put in either during their surgery or at a later date. This helps to boost their self-esteem and confidence, which can help in the healing process. Another option is to have tissue taken from the tummy, back, thighs, or buttocks to rebuild the breast.

To make sure all the cancer is eliminated, treatment often involves surgery that is sometimes combined with chemotherapy, radiation treatments, and/or hormone therapy in an effort to kill any remaining cancer cells. A patient and her doctor will determine what course of treatment is best.

KILLING CANCER WITH CHEMO

Chemotherapy medications are poisons that kill cells. They target cells that are actively dividing. Cancer cells divide much more often than most normal body cells. Some healthy cells do divide actively, though. These include cells in bone marrow, hair, skin, and the lining of the mouth and digestive system. Chemo drugs can't tell the difference between cancer cells and normal cells, so they can damage some normal cells, too. This causes unpleasant side effects such as hair loss, nausea and vomiting, numbness and tingling of the fingers and toes, mouth sores, headache, fatigue, and loss of appetite. The side effects usually are not life-threatening and go away after the treatment is completed.

A woman receives chemotherapy through a needle in her arm.

CHEMOTHERAPY

Chemotherapy—treatment with chemicals—is one of the most effective approaches in fighting cancer. The chemicals used are powerful drugs designed to destroy cancer cells or to interfere with their development. The main objective of chemotherapy is to achieve remission. In remission, there are no longer any symptoms of the disease and laboratory tests show that the tumor has not grown back. That does not mean that the disease is cured, however. Cancer cells may still be present in small numbers somewhere in the body, and they may return sometime in the future. The return of a patient's cancer is called a recurrence. However, a person can stay in remission for months or many years. A recurrence is most likely to develop within five years after treatment is completed. After five years, a recurrence is unlikely, and the disease is considered cured.

Chemotherapy weakens the immune system (the body's defenses). Chemo drugs can kill disease-fighting white blood cells, which divide actively. So patients may get sick easily during treatment. They may have trouble fighting off even a simple cold. A cold could lead to more serious infections, which could become life-threatening. Therefore, patients need to take extra precautions against exposure to germs during treatment.

Chemo is often given after breast cancer surgery to get rid of any cancer cells that may be left behind. When it is given along with surgery, it is called adjuvant chemotherapy. Chemo is almost always urged for patients who have cancer that has spread to the lymph nodes. Sometimes, however, it is given before surgery to decrease the amount of cancer and tissue that needs to be removed.

Many types of chemotherapy are available and given according to a patient's needs. Women with advanced stage cancer are typically given chemo. Some chemotherapy medicines are paclitaxel (brand name Taxol), protein-bound

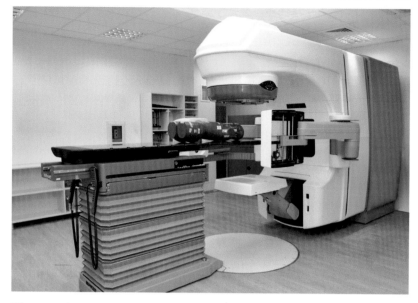

This machine delivers radiation therapy to the area of the body where the cancer is located.

paclitaxel (brand name Abraxane), docetaxel (brand name Taxotere), doxorubicin (brand name Adriamycin), and epirubicin (brand name Ellence). For cancer that has spread, Gemcitabine (brand name Gemzar), capecitabine (brand name Xeloda), vinorelbine (brand name Navelbine), and ixabepilone (brand name Ixempra) are used.

CONTROLLING CANCER WITH RADIATION

Radiation therapy involves the use of high doses of X-rays to kill or damage cancer cells deep inside the body. A special machine is used to direct an X-ray beam to the area of the body that needs treatment. Cancer cells are destroyed because the X-rays damage their ability to divide. As in chemotherapy, some normal cells are also killed in radiation therapy. However, in radiation therapy, the healthy areas can be shielded from the radiation exposure to protect as many normal cells as possible.

A CANCER-FIGHTING TREE?

In the fight against cancer, a compound found in a tree has played a very important role. Scientists have transformed the substance into one of the most effective medications in battling breast and ovarian cancer.

In 1962 the US Department of Agriculture extracted material from the bark of the Pacific yew. The yew is a type of evergreen that grows in the rain forests of the Pacific Northwest, as well as in parts of California, Alaska and Canada. It is slow-growing and can live up to four hundred years. In the 1970s the National Cancer Institute tested the organic material that was not only in the bark but in low levels in the trees' needles. They found that the material helped inhibit cell division in cancers. They called the substance paclitaxel. To make enough of the product, scientists feared thousands of trees would be needed and there simply wouldn't be enough to keep up with demand. By the late 1980s, however, researchers figured out a way to make a synthetic type of paclitaxel. The FDA first approved the use of paclitaxel to treat ovarian cancer in 1992 and then two years later, the FDA approved the drug for use against breast cancer. It was sold under the name Taxol. (Both paclitaxel and Taxol derived their names from the Latin for the Pacific yew—Taxus brevifolia.) Taxol—used alone or in combination with other therapies—became one of the best-selling cancer medications ever made.[6]

The treatment is done every weekday for more than five to six weeks.

Radiation therapy does have some possible dangers. Some people experience mild burns, scarring, nausea, vomiting, and weight loss. Symptoms usually go away within a month or two after treatment. In rare cases, however, there may be a longer-term danger: Radiation therapy can actually cause cancer by producing mutations in the cells' DNA.

Radiation therapy is often used in combination with surgery or chemotherapy. It may be used to reduce the size of the tumor before surgery, to destroy remaining cancer cells after surgery, or in some cases as the main treatment.

A HORMONAL APPROACH

Women who test positive for hormone receptors may be treated with hormone therapy. Tumor cells may contain estrogen receptors, meaning estrogen stimulates their growth. These cells are called estrogen receptor-positive (ER-positive), estrogen-sensitive, or estrogen-responsive. The National Cancer Institute says that about 70 percent of breast cancers are ER-positive.[7] About 65 percent of breast cancers grow in response to another hormone, progesterone. These are said to be PR-positive. The idea behind hormone therapy is to block the hormones from getting to any cancer cells that may be left after surgery. To prevent a recurrence, many patients have hormone therapy after they finish chemotherapy.

The most common type of hormone therapy involves using drugs such as tamoxifen (brand name Nolvadex), raloxifene (brand name Evista), and toremifene (brand name Fareston). Tamoxifen works by attaching to the cancer cell's hormone receptor so that the hormone cannot get to it. Some other drugs, called aromatase inhibitors, work by stopping an enzyme in fat tissue (called aromatase), which in turn lowers estrogen. The end result is the cancer cells cannot get enough of the hormone to grow. These drugs are used to treat early-stage breast cancer. They have become the standard treatment for women who develop breast cancer after menopause. Common aromatase inhibitors are exemestane (brand name Aromasin), letrozole (brand name Femara), and anastrozole (brand name Arimidex).

The most common side effects of hormone therapy are hot flashes, blood clots in the leg veins, and an increase in the risk of uterine cancer. Aromatase inhibitors may also cause joint pain.

Chapter 5

BEATING THE ODDS

W hen Karen Palotas hit age fifty-four, her overall health was sagging. She was pushing two hundred pounds (about 90 kilograms). She rarely exercised and she did not follow a healthy diet. The most exercise she got was walking from the kitchen to the couch with a bag of chips or some other junk food. When she was diagnosed with breast cancer, it was a wake-up call. She decided to not only treat her cancer but to also tackle her weight and eating habits so she could be as healthy as possible.

To eliminate her cancer, she received a double mastectomy followed by six months of chemotherapy and about seven weeks of radiation. She was a breast cancer survivor. Karen then zeroed in on her overall health. She started a new career as an owner of a fitness center.

"You have to care about your health when you're done with your treatment," Karen said. "You change things you're doing wrong, and you look at it as a second shot at life. The day

Working out in a gym is one of many ways to stay fit and lower the risk of cancer.

comes when you decide you want to live and grow old with your husband. To do that, you have to be willing to pick up where the doctors left off."[1]

Karen dedicated her life to getting physically fit. She started a rigorous exercise program and ate healthy foods, which included lots of fresh fruits and vegetables. Eventually, she lost 70 pounds (32 kg) and went from a size 22 to a size 8. "I wasn't this healthy when I was twenty," Karen said.[2]

KEEPING FIT AND EATING RIGHT

Living with cancer is not all about sickness and cancer treatments. It's about staying healthy. In order to do that, cancer patients need to exercise, get enough sleep, and eat the right foods. All these things help to boost the body's immune system, and when the immune system is strong, the patient can fight the cancer more effectively. A strong body can also help a person handle cancer treatments better, as well as the side effects.

During cancer treatment, the patient may feel sick and tired and is probably not in the mood to do much of anything. However, resting too much can weaken muscles, and the body's circulation gets less effective, too. When they're feeling up to it, cancer patients should try to exercise. Physical activity is very important in strengthening the muscles, heart, lungs, and overall circulation. Furthermore, it keeps the whole body strong.

Exercise is also a good way to stay at a healthy weight. As was mentioned earlier, obesity can increase the risk of breast cancer or a recurrence. (Remember, fat tissue produces estrogen, which feeds cancer cells.) People don't need to run two miles a day to get physically fit. Exercise can be gardening, taking long walks, or doing housework—anything that moves the body. A number of studies have shown that women who exercise an hour or more a week after breast cancer treatment have a better survival rate than those who do not exercise at all.

It is important to eat healthy foods, exercise, and get enough rest, particularly when a person with cancer is undergoing treatment.

Exercise is good not only for the body but for the mind as well. When the body is active, chemicals called endorphins work in the brain to produce happy feelings. Exercise can also make people feel good about themselves, giving them a sense of accomplishment and independence.

Getting enough sleep is just as important as getting enough exercise. During the day people use a lot of energy, especially during cancer treatments. Sleep gives the body a chance to rest. While a person is asleep, the body can heal cuts, bruises, and sore muscles. A lack of sleep weakens the body's defenses, which makes it harder to fight off disease germs.

Cancer patients need to watch what they eat as well. A balanced diet that includes a variety of healthy foods will help to strengthen the immune system. It should be high in complex carbohydrates and low in fat, with plenty of protein. Complex carbohydrates help to boost the body's energy level. They may include grains (cereals, pastas, rice, flour, and bran), legumes (beans, lentils, and peas), potatoes, and other vegetables. Some

FOODS THAT MAY HELP FIGHT CANCER

Here are some of the best foods known to have cancer-inhibiting properties:[3]

Broccoli	*Strawberries*
Apples	*Oranges and grapefruits*
Dark green leafy vegetables	*Garlic*
Red and black grapes	*Fish (such as salmon, sardines, and tuna)*
Blueberries	
Cherries	*Black tea, green tea, and coffee*
Ripe tomatoes	

A person who has had cancer needs to eat a variety of nutrient-rich foods to fight off possible infections.

studies have indicated a possible link between fat and cancer, including breast cancer. So doctors recommend that a healthy diet should contain less than 20 to 30 percent fat. Protein is very important because it is needed to build, maintain, and repair cells. During cancer treatment, the body needs enough protein to repair damaged tissues and help to keep the immune system strong.

Dieters typically count the calories in the foods they eat to make sure they don't eat too much. Cancer patients, however, need to count calories to make sure they are eating enough to support their body's needs. Many cancer patients tend to lose weight. They don't just lose stored body fat, they also lose muscle and become weak and tired. Weight loss may become especially severe in the late stages of cancer. This weight loss is partly due to reduced appetite, but changes in the way the body uses food may also play a role. An actively growing tumor uses far more than its share of calories, starving the normal cells. Meanwhile, the body needs extra nutrients to recover after surgery and other treatments.

A healthy diet should also include vitamins and minerals, which are essential for keeping the body systems working properly. Research studies suggest that certain vitamins might help prevent cancer. These are vitamins A, C, and E. They help protect DNA from mutations that may lead to cancer.

Certain foods also contain cancer-fighting chemicals. Fish oil, for example, contains omega-3 fatty acids that can help keep cancer genes under control. "Eat your fruits and veggies" is good advice, too, especially if they are brightly colored. Researchers have discovered that various plant products contain unique phytochemicals (complex chemicals found only in plants) that lower the risk of developing cancer. Some of the cancer-fighting phytochemicals are now available as supplements, but doctors say that the foods in a varied diet are the best way to get them.

BUILD A SUPPORT TEAM OF FAMILY AND FRIENDS

Cancer patients are able to cope much better when they have a good support system of understanding people. Supportive family and friends who stick by the patients no matter what will help them through their battle. However, not all relationships can withstand the stresses involved in battling a disease. For example, sometimes the difficulties can put a serious strain on a marriage.

Support groups can be very helpful for people with cancer. These groups are made up of people who are currently coping with cancer or are cancer survivors. Being able to talk about symptoms, fears, and treatment decisions with people who really understand can be a big help emotionally for someone

Support groups are available for cancer patients as well as their family and friends.

who has recently been diagnosed or is struggling with side effects or setbacks during treatment. Some support groups actually meet in person, but telephone and online support groups are also available. In some cases, support groups include only present and former cancer patients. There are also more formally organized groups that are led by a therapist or other healthcare professional who can provide guidance in coping. The American Cancer Society and other organizations listed at the end of this book sponsor support groups or can provide information about contacting them.

BREAST CANCER PREVENTION

For Angelina Jolie, the possibility of getting breast cancer had been a nagging concern for years. When the actress was just thirty-one years old in 2007, her mother, Marcheline Bertrand, died of breast and ovarian cancer. She was only fifty-six years old, and she had struggled with the disease for almost a decade. Angelina had lost her maternal grandmother to ovarian cancer as well. She was just forty-five when she died. (Later, her aunt Debbie Martin, Marcheline's sister, would succumb to breast cancer at age sixty-one.)

Naturally, Angelina was concerned that she would get breast cancer as well. At age thirty-seven, she didn't have any physical signs of the disease (such as a lump), but because of her family history, she decided to go have genetic testing. Testing revealed that she had the BRCA1 gene mutation. The mutation confirmed that her risk of getting breast cancer was very high. In *The New York Times*, Angelina wrote that her doctors had estimated that her risk of getting breast cancer was 87 percent and that she had a 50 percent chance of getting ovarian cancer.[1]

Angelina Jolie (right) and her mother, Marcheline Bertrand, attend a film premiere in 2001. Marcheline died of ovarian cancer in 2007.

Angelina decided to take proactive measures. She wanted to do whatever she could to be around for her children and her husband, Brad Pitt. She decided to have a double mastectomy, removing the tissue in both her breasts. While it can be a difficult and extreme measure (especially when there is no sign of cancer), the procedure can be a lifesaver. Studies have shown it to be effective in preventing cancer. After consulting with a doctor, she learned she could preserve her natural nipples but remove the breast tissue. In 2013 health care specialists at Stanford University in Palo Alto, California, reported that the nipple can be spared in almost all patients with breast cancer now. Surgeons replaced the removed tissue with implants and reconstructed her breasts so they looked natural.

She announced her decision to the world in hopes of educating more women about breast cancer. Her goal was to raise awareness about treatment options, especially for women with the BRCA mutation. Angelina's story also highlighted that these genetic tests can be expensive, costing upward of three thousand dollars. And reconstructive surgery can also cost a lot—possibly tens of thousands of dollars. So while all women try to choose the best options for their health, cost can be a factor in the decision-making process. The AARP Public Policy Institute found that BRCA testing climbed 40 percent in the week following Angelina's announcement that she tested positive for the BRCA1 gene mutation.[2]

CHECKING FOR BRCA MUTATIONS

With just a simple blood test, a woman can find out if her family history of breast cancer is caused by a BRCA1 or BRCA2 mutation. Some people wonder how this kind of knowledge can really help. If a woman finds out she is carrying a BRCA mutation, she may become worried all the time. She may live her life in fear, just waiting to get breast cancer. Actually, the purpose of genetic testing is to allow a person to take steps to

Angelina Jolie goes shopping with two of her children, Shiloh and Zahara, in 2014.

try to prevent the disease, or to detect it early when it is most treatable.

Usually it is recommended that family members who have had breast cancer be tested for the BRCA mutation. If the test is positive, identifying the gene mutation (BRCA1 or BRCA2) could make it easier for doctors to look for it in other family members.

Anyone who is thinking about genetic testing should seek genetic counseling to go over all the options. People need to remember that testing positive for the BRCA mutation does not mean that they will get breast cancer, but it greatly increases the risk. There are many other things to consider. How would a person handle a positive test result? What are her plans? Knowing about this mutation could help women get tested more regularly. However, some other options are also available that may greatly reduce their risk or actually prevent them from developing breast cancer.

MASTECTOMY AS A PREVENTIVE MEASURE

Some women who test positive for the BRCA mutation, such as Angelina Jolie, may choose a rather extreme method of prevention—getting a double mastectomy. Many people have trouble understanding why someone would want to have a mastectomy when they do not have cancer and may never get cancer. However, people like Angelina see things differently. They see the operation as a way to take control and stop living in fear. It can bring them peace of mind.

Preventive mastectomy is controversial, and some doctors are not willing to perform it on healthy people. Women considering this surgery need to think carefully before making a decision. They should consider their emotional reactions, the financial costs, and possible risks of the operation compared to the benefits of possibly preventing breast cancer.

It is impossible to predict with certainty who will develop breast cancer. Twin sisters Kristen Maurer (left) and Kelly McCarthy were both diagnosed with breast cancer several years ago. Neither tested positive for the BRCA mutation.

HORMONE THERAPIES TO WARD OFF CANCER

Another option for women with a high risk for breast cancer is taking tamoxifen. Remember that this drug works by preventing cancer cells from picking up estrogen. It also helps reduce the risk of developing breast cancer. (It works only for types of breast cancer sensitive to hormones, however.)

Women who have already had children may choose to have their ovaries surgically removed. The ovaries make most of the body's estrogen. With the estrogen level greatly reduced, the risk of breast cancer is lowered.

Chapter 7

THE FUTURE OF BREAST CANCER

The pink ribbon is perhaps the most recognizable symbol for breast cancer awareness in the United States. In early 1992 newspaper columnist Liz Smith wrote about Charlotte Haley, a sixty-eight-year-old woman who created her own peach-colored ribbons for breast cancer. Her grandmother, sister, and daughter had all had breast cancer. Charlotte included a card with each ribbon that read: The National Cancer Institute annual budget is $1.8 billion, only 5 percent goes for cancer prevention. Help us wake up our legislators and America by wearing this ribbon. She handed out cards to people in supermarkets and also sent them to popular columnists and other well-known women.

RACE FOR THE CURE

Thousands of participants in cities across the country walk or run in the Susan G. Komen Breast Cancer Foundation's annual Race for the Cure, which raises money for breast cancer awareness and research. It has been called the world's largest and most successful education and fundraising event for breast cancer ever created.

Runners and walkers participate in the 2014 Race for the Cure West Palm Beach, Florida.

The pink ribbon has become a worldwide symbol for breast cancer awareness.

Around the same time, Alexandra Penney, then the editor of *Self* magazine, was hoping to create a breast cancer ribbon for the magazine's Breast Cancer Awareness Month issue.

The magazine lawyers suggested that she change the color of the ribbon from Charlotte Haley's peach. The new color, they decided, would be pink, a color that could represent all women. In fall 1992, Estée Lauder makeup counters handed out 1.5 million ribbons, along with a card that described how to do a proper breast self-exam. They also collected over 200,000 signatures on letters asking the White House to increase the money for breast cancer research.

One year later, the pink ribbon had become a national symbol for breast cancer. More and more companies joined the fight against breast cancer, helping to raise millions of dollars. Between 1991 and 1996, federal funding for breast cancer increased sharply, from $90 million a year to over $550 million. In addition, the American Cancer Society found that the number of women who were getting yearly mammograms and clinical breast exams had more than doubled during the 1990s.[1]

Pink ribbons are still a symbol for breast cancer awareness. Raising awareness has been an important focus for breast cancer organizations. Many women are now getting diagnosed earlier and therefore have a better chance for survival. Another important result has been raising more money for developing better tests and treatments.

TARGETED MEDICATIONS

One of the most promising areas of cancer research today is the development of drugs designed to kill cells of a particular kind of cancer. They work by zeroing in on the target—the cancer—and killing only cancer cells, not normal cells. Other cancer treatments, such as chemotherapy and radiation, kill both cancer cells and healthy cells, which results in terrible side effects. Since healthy cells remain unharmed when targeted drugs are

Around the world, researchers are working to develop new treatments and cures for breast cancer.

used, there are fewer side effects. Many scientists are calling these targeted drugs the "wave of the future."

One of the most promising areas of cancer research today is the development of drugs designed to kill cells of a particular kind of cancer.

Researchers have already identified a number of genes linked with the development of breast cancer. The BRCA1 and BRCA2 genes were discussed earlier. In addition, it has been found that 25 to 30 percent of breast cancer patients have extra copies of a gene called HER2 (hormone epidermal growth factor receptor 2). This status makes cells sensitive to human growth factor, a hormone controlling growth.[2] The extra copies of the gene result in uncontrolled cell growth—cancer. Identifying cancer genes gives researchers a way of making drugs that target these specific genes. A drug called trastuzumab (brand name Herceptin) has already been developed to block the effects of the HER2 gene. It targets only cells with extra copies of the gene, leaving healthy cells alone. This way it can stop tumor growth without producing the typical side effects of chemotherapy drugs. Doctors can now test for HER2 genes and thus find out exactly which patients will get the best results from the drug.

In 1998 the Food and Drug Administration (FDA) approved trastuzumab for treating patients with advanced breast cancer. Even after the cancer had metastasized, patients who received trastuzumab along with chemotherapy survived up to one third longer than those who had only chemotherapy. In 2013 research demonstrated that trastuzumab combined with other medication may be effective in extending lives of those with advanced breast cancer.[3] A study from the Mayo Clinic in 2014 showed that trastuzumab added to

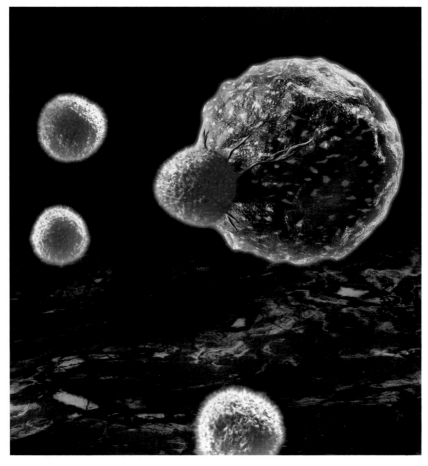

This digital image shows T cells attacking a cancer cell. These "killer" T cells are one promising aspect of breast cancer research.

standard chemotherapy boosted ten-year survival rates from 75 percent to 84 percent.[4]

Trastuzumab is injected directly into the blood. The FDA approved the drug lapatinib (brand name Tykerb) for certain postmenopausal women with breast cancer that has spread. This medication also targets the HER2 gene but can be taken in pill form. This drug can pass from the bloodstream into the brain. According to early studies, when Tykerb is given with chemotherapy, the cancer is less likely to spread to the brain.[5]

More recently, in 2012 and 2013, pertuzumab (brand name Perjeta)—another HER2-targeting medication—got the green light for treating early stage breast cancer before surgery and advanced HER2-positive breast cancer.

In 2012 the FDA gave their approval for a medication called everolimus (brand name Affinitor) to treat advanced hormone-receptor–positive breast cancer in women who have gone through menopause. In human trials, this drug helped hormone therapy drugs work better.

Some breast cancers are identified as "triple-negative." About 15 percent of breast cancer patients have this type of cancer, according to the National Breast Cancer Foundation. These cancer cells do not have any of the three most common receptors known to feed breast cancer—estrogen, progesterone, or HER2. Without these receptors, this type of cancer does not respond to hormones and drugs that target HER2. Chemotherapy has been shown to be an effective treatment option.[6]

Meanwhile, several groups of researchers are working on vaccines that can make the patient's own white blood cells attack and kill breast cancer cells. One experimental vaccine uses the protein made by the HER2 gene to train a special kind of white blood cells called killer T cells. In 2014 researchers at Washington School of Medicine in St. Louis had promising results with a vaccine that helped the immune system attack tumor cells and slow cancer growth. The vaccine prompts the

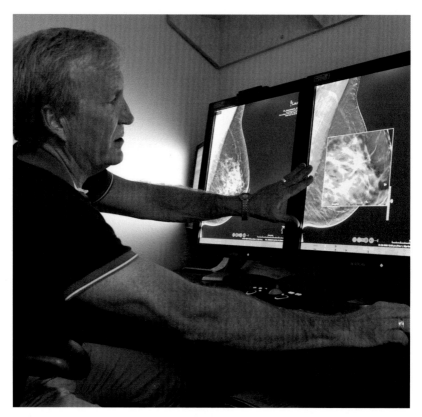

A radiologist shows the difference between a traditional mammogram and a newer, 3-D digital mammogram. The digital mammogram is able to display much greater detail.

immune system to zero in on mammaglobin, which is found in 80 percent of breast cancers. Some preliminary trials on human patients have been promising.[7]

Other new medications being developed include anti-angiogenesis drugs. Cancers depend on blood vessels to feed them. These new types of medications are designed to block cancer growth by stopping new blood vessels from forming.

ADVANCED SCREENING TECHNIQUES

Mammography has been the standard screening test for breast cancer since the 1960s. Mammograms have saved lives by helping to detect cancers earlier, while they are more easily treated. However, mammograms can miss very early breast cancers—those too small to detect or hidden by dense breast tissue. They also give a number of "false positives"—findings that look like cancer but turn out to be benign. Women who receive such results need to have extra tests or even surgery. Doctors would like to have better ways of testing. They want to be able to detect breast cancer even earlier and spare women worry and expense by reducing false-positive results.

Computers are now playing a big role in the development of new mammography techniques. In digital mammography, a computer turns the X-ray picture into a digital image instead of recording it on X-ray film. Changing the magnification, brightness, or contrast of the digital image brings out details that would not be noticed on an X-ray film. This is especially helpful in finding tumors in younger women with dense breast tissue. Digital images can be stored much more easily than films, and they can be sent electronically to other locations to be viewed by other experts. A further advance is computer-aided detection and diagnosis (CAD). A computer program is used to point out suspicious areas to be checked more closely by a radiologist.

THE BEAUTY OF BREAST CANCER AWARENESS

For about twenty years, Elizabeth Hurley has been the face of Estée Lauder's breast cancer awareness campaign, and as an actress over the age of forty she has stressed the importance of regular breast screening. Elizabeth says, "Breast cancer is being detected at an earlier, more treatable stage these days, largely because women are taking more preventive measures like self-exams and regular mammograms. And treatment is getting better, too." Elizabeth appreciates that we live in an age that we talk about breast cancer and share information to help women get the help they need. When her grandmother died of the disease in 1992, she says that people still didn't talk about it much. "Breast cancer was a word that was only whispered," she says. "Today, we shout about breast cancer from the rooftops."

Some mammograms may be "contrast-enhanced." Using an iodine contrast agent, the imaging equipment highlights and enhances area where lesions or tumors are likely to exist.

Molecular breast imaging, developed at the Mayo Clinic, uses a specially designed "gamma camera." It takes pictures of tiny tumors that are too small to be detected by a mammogram. Women with suspicious findings on mammograms are injected with tiny amounts of a radioactive chemical, too small to cause any harm. The radioactive chemical gives off gamma rays and tends to build up in cells that are very active—such as cancer cells. The researchers say their technique is much better than mammography in detecting cancer in women with dense breast tissue.[8]

So many advances in cancer have depended on a growing understanding of genes. In recent years, a technique called gene expression profiling has been developed as a method for predicting a woman's breast cancer risk. The Mayo Clinic says that gene expression profiling analyzes patterns of many different genes within cancer cells. These genes are the codes or blueprints that tell the cells how to function. The gene patterns can help predict how likely breast cancer will recur after initial therapy. Two such tests are Oncotype DX and MammaPrint. This is a new approach to analyzing risk—the effectiveness of gene expression profiling is still being studied and fine-tuned.[9]

THE FIGHT GOES ON

Cancer diagnosis and treatment has come a long way since the 1970s. Advances have led to more people who have had breast cancer living disease-free for longer periods of time. The American Cancer Society reported in 2015 that there were about 2.8 million breast cancer survivors in the United States.[10] The Centers for Disease Control and Prevention stated that death rates from breast cancer across the country have dropped two percent each year from 2001 to 2010.[11] The organization

More women are surviving breast cancer every year thanks to greater awareness, early detection, and advances in treatments.

attributes these strong numbers to early detection, increased awareness, and better treatments.

Although steps are being made in the right direction, the disease continues to be a major health problem. The National Cancer Institute has predicted that there will be about 232,000 new cases of breast cancer among women in 2015 and about 40,000 deaths due to breast cancer in the United States.[12] So while great strides continue to be taken in the fight against the disease, there is still a long road ahead toward eliminating breast cancer.

I just found out my mom has breast cancer. Does that mean that she's going to die?

These days, more and more people are surviving breast cancer. If your mom's cancer was found early, she has a better than 90 percent chance of surviving. If the cancer has spread to other parts of the body, the condition is much more serious, but there are still treatments that may help.

The chemotherapy treatments are making my mom really sick and miserable. How is it helping her get better?

The drugs are killing the cancer cells, but they are also harming some healthy body cells that normally divide actively, such as those in the hair follicles and in the lining of the stomach and intestines. Your mom will feel better once the cancer cells have been wiped out and the treatments can be stopped.

Both my mom and my grandmother had breast cancer. Does that mean that I'll get it, too?

Not necessarily. The genes you inherit can increase your risk of getting cancer, but your lifestyle and environment also play important roles. Even if you have inherited genes linked with breast cancer, you may never get the disease. If you have an increased risk, however, it is important to do monthly breast self-exams and have regular checkups. Then if breast cancer does develop, it is more likely to be detected at an early, treatable stage.

Are people with bigger breasts more likely to get breast cancer?

No. The size of breasts have nothing to do with whether or not a person will get breast cancer. Everybody has breast tissue. Even men can get breast cancer (although it is very rare). However, women with larger breasts may have a harder time trying to feel for a lump.

Do breast implants cause breast cancer?

No, but they may make it more difficult to find a lump. When getting a mammogram, women with implants should tell the technician about them. The technician will need to take extra pictures to get different views.

At what age should girls start doing breast self-exams?

Even though most breast cancer cases are found in women over forty, it is best to start doing breast self-exams at around twenty years old. This way, a woman can become familiar with her breasts, in the way they look and feel. Then as she gets older, she will notice when something doesn't feel right, such as finding an unusual lump.

I'm afraid I might have breast cancer. What are the signs?

Often there are no signs of early breast cancer. Sometimes there may be a lump, an area of thickening, or a dimpling in the breast. But remember, even if you have one of these symptoms, it does not mean that you have breast cancer. Consult your doctor.

What's the big deal about a girl starting puberty early, like nine years old? What does that have to do with breast cancer?

When a girl starts puberty, her body releases a lot of hormones, including estrogen, which has been linked to breast cancer. Scientists have found that estrogen feeds cancer cells, helping them to grow and multiply. The more exposure a woman has to estrogen during her lifetime, the greater her chances of developing breast cancer. So the risk is increased the earlier she starts puberty and the later she starts menopause (the time at which a woman stops getting her monthly period).

I read that Angelina Jolie had a family history of breast cancer. She had genetic testing and found out that she had a gene mutation that made her more likely to get breast cancer. I also have a family history of breast cancer. Should I get genetic tests to see if I have this mutation?

Having a gene mutation that is linked to breast cancer is relatively rare. Most cancer experts advise that genetic testing only be done when a person's family history suggests the possible presence of a mutation. Since you do have a family history of breast cancer, you may want to talk to your doctor about the possibility of getting tested.

I heard that wearing a bra regularly can lead to breast cancer. Is this true?

There have been no studies that show any link between wearing a bra and getting breast cancer.

Timeline of Breast Cancer

1600—BC Egyptians record earliest descriptions of breast cancer.

400—BC Greek physician Hippocrates uses the term *cancer* to describe a group of diseases involving tumors, lumps, and bumps.

AD—100s Greek physician Leonides performs the first recorded surgical removal of the breast (mastectomy).

1700— French physician Claude Gendron publishes a book explaining that cancers are solid structures that form from body tissues such as nerves, glands, or lymphatic vessels.

1757— French surgeon Henri Le Dran says that cancer is a local disease that first spreads to the lymph nodes, then to the lymphatic system, and from there to other parts of the body.

Mid—1800s German physician Johannes Müller reports that cancerous tumors are made up of abnormal cells that look different from normal cells under a microscope.

1867— British surgeon Charles Moore introduces the radical mastectomy, a procedure that removes the breast, chest muscle, and lymph nodes.

1894— American surgeon William Halsted publishes a report that helps to make the radical mastectomy standard treatment for breast cancer.

1895— German physicist Wilhelm Conrad Roentgen discovers X-rays.

1896— Emile Grubbe becomes the first person to use X-rays to treat breast cancer.

1906— British surgeon W. Sampson Handley becomes the first to use radiation therapy.

1913— German surgeon Albert Salomon runs X-ray studies of breast tissue from 3,000 mastectomies. His results form the basis for mammography.

1922— Geoffrey Keynes introduces lumpectomy plus radiation as a breast cancer treatment.

1930s— Mammography begins to be used for diagnosis of breast cancer.

1946— Nitrogen mustard is used for cancer chemotherapy.

1960s— Mammograms have proven to be an effective diagnostic tool.

1969— The first X-ray machines used only for mammography are introduced.

1975— Modified radical mastectomy becomes the preferred treatment for breast cancer.

1985— Researchers identify the HER2 gene as linked to cancer.

1990— The National Cancer Institute declares lumpectomy plus radiation as the preferred treatment for early-stage breast cancer. Researchers identify BRCA1 as the first gene linked to breast cancer.

1998— Tamoxifen is the first drug used in the prevention of breast cancer. FDA approves Herceptin, which tar gets the HER2 gene, for the treatment of advanced breast cancer.

2005— The BRCA2 gene is found in other types of cancer in addition to breast cancer. Clinical trials show that Herceptin prevents recurrence in 50 percent of women with early-stage breast cancer.

2006— Clinical trials show that raloxifene (Evista) is as effective as tamoxifen in preventing breast cancer, with fewer side effects.

2007— Ixabepilone (brand name Ixempra) is approved by FDA to block or slow tumors in women with advanced breast cancer who no longer respond to chemotherapy. Lapatinib (Tykerb) gains FDA approval to be used with patients with HER2-positive cancer who no longer respond to Herceptin.

The American Cancer Society recommends routing MRI screening for women at high risk of developing breast cancer.

Studies show that lower use of hormone replacement therapy in postmenopausal women linked to lower breast cancer rate.

2008— FDA approves bevacizumab (brand name Avastin) used with paclitaxel (brand name Taxol) for newly diagnosed advanced breast cancers. Some research questions benefits.

2009— Novel PARP inhibitors show promise against hard-to-treat triple-negative breast cancer Preventive surgery shows to lower breast cancer and ovarian cancer risk in women with mutated BRCA genes.

2011— Aromatase inhibitors lower likelihood of cancer among high risk women.

2012— Combo of pertuzumab (brand name Perjeta) and Herceptin, along with chemotherapy, shown to significantly slow cancer in women with advanced can cer and HER2 mutation.

Next generation of trastuzumab shown to help women with HER2-positive breast cancer live longer. Medication is called trastuzumab emtansine (T-DM1; brand name Kadcyla).

2013— AARP Public Policy Institute finds that BRCA testing climbs 40 percent in week following Angelina Jolie's announcement that she tested positive for BRCA1 gene mutation.

Chapter 1. A Concern for All Women

1. Samantha Harris, "About Samantha," *Gotta Make Lemonade*, accessed February 15, 2015, http://gottamakelemonade. com/about-samantha.

Chapter 2. The Unspoken Disease Gets a Voice

1. "Breast Cancer Statistics," Susan G. Komen, last modified January 22, 2015, http://ww5.komen.org/BreastCancer/ Statistics.html.
2. Janet R. Osuch et al., "A Historical Perspective on Breast Cancer Activism in the United States: From Educational Support to Partnership in Scientific Research," *Journal of Women's Health* 21, no. 3 (March 2012). doi:10.1089/ jwh.2011.2862.
3. Ibid.
4. "New Attitudes Ushered In by Betty Ford," *New York Times*, October 17, 1987, 9.
5. "Breast Cancer Risk in American Women," *National Cancer Institute*, last modified September 24, 2012, http://www. cancer.gov/types/breast/risk-fact-sheet
6. Richard A. Evans, *The Cancer Breakthrough You've Never Heard Of* (Murdock, 2001).
7. The National Surgical Adjuvant Breast and Bowel Project (NSABP), "An Historical Overview," accessed February 15, 2015, http://www.nsabp.pitt.edu.
8. Ibid.

Chapter 3. Understanding Breast Cancer

1. Stone Phillips, "Melissa's Brave Comeback," *MSNBC.com*, February 22, 2005, http://www.msnbc.msn.com/ id/6994469.

2. Stone Phillips, "Melissa Etheridge's Anthem of Hope," *MSNBC.com*, October 16, 2005, http://www.msnbc.msn .com/id/9673481/.

3. "Risk of Developing Breast Cancer," *BreastCancer.org*, accessed February 15, 2015, http://www.breastcancer.org/ symptoms/understand_bc/risk/understanding.

4. "Breast Cancer in Men," American Cancer Society, last modified February 26, 2015, http://www.cancer.org/cancer/ breastcancerinmen/detailedguide/breast-cancer-in-men-key-statistics.

5. "Breast Cancer Risk by Age," *Centers for Disease Control and Prevention*, last modified September 26, 2014, http:// www.cdc.gov/cancer/breast/statistics/age.htm.

6. "Invasive Ductal Carcinoma" *National Breast Cancer Foundation*, accessed February 15, 2015, http://www .nationalbreastcancer.org/invasive-ductal-carcinoma.

7. "BRCA1 and BRCA2: Cancer Risk and Genetic Testing," *National Cancer Institute*, January 2014. http://www.cancer .gov/cancertopics/factsheet/Risk/BRCA.

Chapter 4. Detecting, Then Treating

1. Alex Tresniowski and Laura Figueroa, "For the Love of Mom," *People Magazine*, March 27, 2006, 163-164.

2. Bob Harig, "Golfer, 13, Fulfills Her Mother's Dream," *St. Petersburg Times*, April 28, 2006, http://articles. chicagotribune.com/2006-04-28/sports/0604280170_1_ kelly-jo-dowd-dakoda-dowd-mike-dowd.

3. Anne Lane, "Benign Breast Lumps," *HealthDay*, last modified March 2014, http://consumer.healthday.com/ encyclopedia/breast-cancer-7/breast-cancer-news-94/ benign-breast-lumps-644244.html.

4. Sarah M. Friedewald, "Breast Cancer Screening Using Tomosynthesis in Combination With Digital Mammography," *The Journal of the American Medical*

Association 311, no. 24 (2014): 2499-2507. doi:10.1001/jama.2014.6095.

5. "Mammograms," *National Cancer Institute*, accessed March 10, 2015, http://www.cancer.gov/cancertopics/types/breast/mammograms-fact-sheet

6. "Success Story: Taxol," *National Cancer Institute*, accessed February 15, 2015, http://dtp.nci.nih.gov/timeline/flash/success_stories/S2_taxol.htm.

7. "Hormone Therapy for Breast Cancer," *National Cancer Institute*, accessed March 10, 2015, http://www.cancer.gov/cancertopics/types/breast/breast-hormone-therapy-fact-sheet.

Chapter 5. Beating the Odds

1. Meg Nugent, "Recovery in Motion," *The Star-Ledger* (Newark, N.J.), October 31, 2005, 25, 32.

2. Ibid.

3. "AICR's Foods That Fight Cancer," *American Institute for Cancer Research*, October 2014, http://www.aicr.org/foods-that-fight-cancer/.

Chapter 6. Breast Cancer Prevention

1. Angelina Jolie, "My Medical Choice," *The New York Times,* May 14, 2013, http://www.nytimes.com/2013/05/14/opinion/my-medical-choice.html?_r=1

2. Ibid.

Chapter 7. The Future of Breast Cancer

1. Pam Stephan, "Breast Cancer and the Pink Ribbon Symbol," *AboutHealth,* last modified August 14, 2014, http://breastcancer.about.com/od/supportineveryway/a/pink-ribbon-history.htm.

2. "A Story of Discovery: HER2's Genetic Link to Breast Cancer Spurs Development of New Treatments," *National Cancer Institute*, accessed February 15, 2015, http://www

.cancer.gov/aboutnci/servingpeople/cancer-research-progress/discovery/HER2.

3. "Living With Metastatic Cancer," *Susan G. Komen*, January 29, 2014, http://ww5.komen.org/KomenPerspectives/ Living-with-metastatic-breast-cancer- %28January-2014%29.html.

4. Edith Perez et al, "Trastuzumab Plus Adjuvant Chemotherapy for Human Epidermal Growth Factor Receptor 2–Positive Breast Cancer: Planned Joint Analysis of Overall Survival From NSABP B-31 and NCCTG N9831," *Journal of Clinical Oncology*, October 2014, http://jco.ascopubs.org/ content/early/2014/10/14/JCO.2014.55.5730.abstract.

5. "Metastatic Breast Cancer," *Susan G. Komen*, last modified February 10, 2015, http://ww5.komen.org/BreastCancer/ RecommendedTreatmentsforMetastaticBreastCancer.html.

6. "Triple Negative Breast Cancer," *National Breast Cancer Foundation, Inc.*, accessed June 5, 2015, http://www. nationalbreastcancer.org/triple-negative-breast-cancer.

7. "Breast Cancer Vaccine Shows Promise in Early Trial," *MedlinePlus*, December 2, 2014, http://www.nlm.nih.gov/ medlineplus/news/fullstory_149753.html.

7. Sam Smith, "New Breast Exam Nearly Quadruples Detection of Invasive Breast Cancers in Women with Dense Breast Tissue," *Mayo Clinic*, January 23, 2015, http:// newsnetwork.mayoclinic.org/discussion/new-breast-exam-nearly-quadruples-detection-of-invasive-breast-cancers-in-women-with-dense-breast-ti.

8. "Gene Expression Profiling for Breast Cancer: What Is It?" *Mayo Clinic*, July 10, 2012, http://www.mayoclinic.org/ diseases-conditions/breast-cancer/expert-answers/gene-expression-profiling/FAQ-20058144.

9. "What Are rhe Key Statistics About Breast Cancer?" *American Cancer Society*, last modified February 26, 2015, http://www.cancer.org/cancer/breastcancer/detailedguide/ breast-cancer-key-statistics.

10. "Breast Cancer Trends," *Centers for Disease Control and Prevention*, last modified February 6, 2015, http://www .cdc.gov/cancer/breast/statistics/trends.htm.

11. Rebecca L. Siegel, Kimberly D. Miller, and Ahmedin Jemal, "Cancer statistics, 2015," *Wiley Online Library*, January 5, 2015. doi:10.3322/caac.21254.

GLOSSARY

adjuvant therapy—A treatment that is given in addition to primary treatment. Often chemotherapy given after surgery is called adjuvant.

anesthetics—Drugs that temporarily numb the body and block feelings of pain.

antiseptics—Chemicals that kill disease-causing germs.

axillary nodes—Lymph nodes in the armpits.

benign—Pertaining to a noncancerous tumor.

biopsy—The removal of a small sample of tissue, cells, or fluid for microscopic examination to check for abnormalities and establish a diagnosis.

blood vessels—Tubular structures that carry blood to nearly all the cells of the body. They include arteries, veins, and capillaries.

BRCA genes—Breast cancer genes that help in breast growth and protect against breast cancer. Mutations in these genes significantly increase the risk for getting breast cancer.

capillaries—Tiny, thin-walled blood vessels.

carcinogens—Cancer-causing chemicals, such as those found in cigarettes, certain foods, and industrial materials.

carcinoma—Cancers that start in epithelial tissue (covering and lining tissues). Examples include cancers of the lungs, breast, ovaries, prostate, and stomach.

cell—The smallest basic functional unit or building block of life.

chemotherapy—The use of drugs to treat diseases by killing invading germs or cancerous cells or by stopping their growth and reproduction.

cyst—A fluid-filled sac. Noncancerous cysts are often found in the breast.

DNA (deoxyribonucleic acid)—The substance that carries the hereditary instructions for making proteins.

ducts—Hollow tubes that carry a fluid. Ducts in the breast carry milk.

estrogen—A female sex hormone.

fibrocystic breast changes—Lumps in the breast that may become larger and painful at certain times of the month, due to the hormonal ups and downs of the menstrual cycle.

gene—A chemical unit containing coded instructions to make a protein; genes carry hereditary traits from one generation to the next.

gene expression profiling—a measurement of activity of thousands of genes. It can be used to better understand patterns of many different genes within cancer cells and help predict cancer growth.

glands—Structures in the body that release chemicals.

HER2 gene—A gene that helps in normal health breast cell growth and repair. In 25 to 30 percent of breast cancer patients, the gene is not working properly and makes too many extra copies of itself, leading to abnormal cell growth.

hormones—Chemicals released into the bloodstream that help to control and regulate the body's activities.

immune system—The body's defenses against invading germs or foreign cells and tissues.

lobes—A collection of lobules.

lobules—Tiny saclike glands that produce milk during breast-feeding.

lumpectomy—A surgical procedure in which the breast tumor is removed along with some normal tissue around it.

lymphatic system—A network of vessels that return filtered lymph (fluid drained from the tissues after leaking out of capillaries) to the circulatory system.

lymph nodes—Small structures scattered along the lymphatic system; they contain disease-fighting cells.

malignant—Pertaining to a cancerous tumor.

mammaglobin—A protein found almost exclusively in breast tissue and expressed in up to 80 percent of breast cancers.

mammogram—An X-ray of the breast.

mastectomy—A surgical procedure to remove one or both breasts to keep the cancer from spreading to other parts of the body.

menopause—A time in which a woman stops having her monthly period, and the ovaries no longer produce estrogen.

menstrual cycle—A process that prepares the female body for a possible pregnancy. It includes the production and release of hormones and the maturing and release of an ovum (egg), and thickening of the lining of the uterus.

metastasis—The spread of cancer cells to different parts of the body, where they form new tumors.

mutation—A chemical change in a gene, which may produce a new trait that can be inherited.

obesity—Extreme overweight

ovaries—A pair of oval-shaped female sex organs in which eggs and hormones are produced.

progesterone—A female hormone that is key to regulating ovulation and menstruation.

puberty—The period of rapid growth and changes in the body as the sex organs mature and become capable of reproduction.

radiation therapy—The use of high doses of X-rays or other radiations to kill cancer cells deep inside the body.

radical mastectomy—Surgical removal of the breast, together with the underlying muscles and axillary lymph nodes, to prevent spread of breast cancer to other parts of the body.

recurrence—Return of an illness.

remission—A lessening or disappearance of disease symptoms and signs.

sex hormones—Chemicals that are produced naturally by the ovaries (in females) or testes (in males) and help to control and coordinate the normal functioning of the body's cells, organs, and systems.

testicles—Male sex glands.

testosterone—Male sex hormones.

tumor—A solid mass formed from a buildup of cells.

American Cancer Society
cancer.org
Provides support and education for individuals with cancer and is dedicated to finding treatments and cures for cancer.

American Institute for Cancer Research (AICR)
aicr.org
Focuses on cancer prevention and treatment through diet and physical activity.

Breastcancer.org
breastcancer.org
Provides up-to-date information about breast cancer to help patients make informed decisions about treatment.

Cancer Care–National Office
cancercare.org
Offers counseling, support groups, education, and financial assistance for cancer patients and their families.

Centers for Disease Control and Prevention
National Center for Chronic Disease Prevention and Health Promotion
Division of Cancer Prevention and Control
cdc.gov/cancer
Provides detailed information about cancer prevention, research, data, and publications.

The Susan G. Komen Breast Cancer Foundation
komen.org
Dedicated to raising money and support for breast cancer research and programs.

FURTHER READING

Cohen, Deborah, and Robert M. Gelfand. *Just Get Me Through This!* New York: Kensington, 2011.

Link, John. *The Breast Cancer Survival Manual, Fifth Edition.* New York: Holt Paperbacks, 2012.

Mills, Wendy. *Positively Beautiful.* New York: Bloomsbury USA Children's Publishing, 2015.

Parks, Peggy J. *Breast Cancer.* San Diego: ReferencePoint Press, 2014.

Silver, Maya, and Marc Silver. *My Parent Has Cancer and It Really Sucks.* Naperville, Ill.: Sourcebooks, 2013.

INDEX